THE DISPUTATION

THE DISPUTATION

By Hyam Maccoby

Introduction by Dr Jonathan Sacks

CALDER PUBLICATIONS
LONDON

First published by Calder Publications UK Ltd, London. 2001

© Hyam Maccoby 2001

ALL RIGHTS RESERVED
ISBN 07145 43179

The right of Hyam Maccoby to be identified as author of this work has been asserted by him in accordance with the Copyright Design and Patents Act 1988.

All performing rights in this play are strictly reserved and application for performance should be addressed to Brian Daniels, Pluto Productions, The New End Theatre, 27 New End, London NW3 1JD

British Library Cataloguing in Publication Data
A catalogue record for this book is available from the British Library

Apart from any fair dealing for the purpose of research or private study, or criticism or review, as permitted under the Copyright Design and Patents Act, 1988, this publication may not be reproduced, stored in or introduced in a retrieval system or transmitted, in any form or by any means, electronic, mechanical, photocopying, recording or otherwise, without the prior written permission of the publisher

Typeset by Newton Design & Print Ltd, UK, www.newtondp.co.uk

Printed by Watkiss Studios Ltd, UK

The Disputation

The Disputation is Hyam Maccoby's powerful reconstruction of one of the most fascinating, though ultimately tragic, encounters between Jews and Christians in the Middle Ages.

It is hard, at this distance of time, to recapture the mood of that dark and dangerous age. Beginning with the first crusade in 1096, when Jewish communities in Northern France and the Rhineland were massacred, Christian attitudes towards Jews turned sporadically violent and vicious. In 1144, in Norwich, the famous 'Blood Libel' made its first appearance, and in subsequent centuries Jews were accused of ritual murder, desecrating the host and poisoning wells. These accusations spread from county to county, bringing bloodshed in their wake. In 1290 England became the first medieval nation to expel its Jews, and this too was repeated throughout Europe during the next two centuries.

Beginning in 1240 in the wake of Pope Gregory IX's ban on the Talmud, a series of public disputations took place in which Jews were invited not so much to defend their faith as to concede the superior power of Christianity as the prelude to their conversion. Hyam Maccoby has himself provided us with a gripping account of the three occasions of which a written record has survived (Paris 1240, Barcelona 1263 and Tortosa 1413-14 in his excellent book *Judaism on Trial*). Of these by far the most remarkable was the Barcelona Disputation, which forms the subject of the play. Two factors made it unusual. The first was the presence of one of the true giants of medieval Jewry, Rabbi Moses ben Nahman (Nahmanides), talmudist, Bible commentator, physician, philosopher and mystic, one of rabbinical Judaism's most subtle and expansive minds. The other was the relative freedom of speech granted to the Jewish side by King James of Aragon, one of the more tolerable and likeable rulers of that age. As Maccoby points out, the real dilemma facing Nahmanides was whether it was better to win or to lose. Losing meant betraying his faith and demoralising his people. Winning (and thus humiliating his Christian opponent) meant almost certain reprisals against himself and the Jewish community. It is hard to be sure exactly what happened. Two accounts, one Christian, one written by Nahmanides himself, exist, and needless to say they paint two very different pictures. The subsequent facts, though seem reasonably clear. Initially the king was warm towards Nahmanides, awarding him a prize of 300 gold coins. Two years later, a Dominican backlash resulted in his exile at the age of 70. He travelled to Jerusalem where, in one of the last great acts of his career, he reconstructed the Jewish community there, establishing a yeshiva and founding a synagogue that still bears his name.

Maccoby's play is not intended to be a precise historical account. In part it is a dramatic reconstruction of the great themes that have driven his own work in a series of strongly argued and controversial books: the theological dimensions of anti-Semitism, the demonisation of the Jews in Christian literature, and the complex psychology of guilt and blame. The courage and dignity shown by Nahmanides throughout the play is, one feels, Maccoby's own testimony to his love of Judaism as a religion of this-worldly redemption, which refuses to say that the Messiah has come into a world still riven by injustice and war, and which equally resists a view of mankind as corrupted by the original sin and thus in need of salvation. We are what we choose to be, still summoned by Moses to 'Choose Life'.

It took a long time for a more expansive air to prevail in Europe. In the centuries after the Barcelona Disputation, the condition of the Jews in Spain continued to worsen. There were anti-Jewish riots and forced conversions, the Spanish Inquisition and the birth of a racially anti-Semitic doctrine known as Limpieza de sangre (purity of blood) culminating in the Spanish Expulsion of 1492, one of the deepest traumas of the Jewish Middle Ages. In the end it took the holocaust for a new Christian Doctrine to emerge, one that finally conceded the integrity of Jews and Judaism as embodying the first and still unbroken covenant between God and a people.

Chief Rabbi Dr Jonathan Sacks.

CAST OF CHARACTERS

(in order of appearance)
Raymond de Penaforte, Dominican leader
Queen Yolanda of Aragon
King James I of Aragon
Don Alconstantini, a Jewish courtier
Attendant
Pablo Christiani, a Dominican friar, convert from Judaism
Consuelo, the King's mistress
Judith, daughter of Rabbi Moses
Rabbi Moses ben Nachman
King's Officer

Time   1263

Place   Various locations in the Court of King James of Aragon and in the city of Barcelona.

The Disputation was produced by Pluto productions and first performed at The New End Theatre, Hampstead in April 2001 with the following cast.

Raymond de Penaforte	Robert Rietti
Queen Yolanda	Hildegard Neil
King James	William Russell
Attendant Officer	Nicholas Pitman
Don Alconstantini	Jonathan Melia
Pablo Christiani	Christian Bradley
Consuelo	Josephine Welcome
Moses Ben Nachman	Leonard Fenton
Judith	Maxine Gregory
Director	Robert Kalfin

Prior to the British production The Disputation had successful performances in Los Angeles, New York and Miami.

ACT I.

BOYS' CHOIR.

VOICE. You have been found guilty of speaking against the throne of Aragon. On this 25th day of June in the year 1263, by decree of the King of Aragon, James the Conqueror, your punishment, so as to remind you for ever of your betrayal, is to have your offending tongue removed. Forgive me, Father.

THE COURT OF KING JAMES OF ARAGON. RAYMOND DE PENAFORTE.

ENTER QUEEN YOLANDA.

QUEEN YOLANDA. Tell me there is something I can do, Raymond.

RAYMOND DE PENAFORTE.. Your Majesty, I would be remiss if I did not tell you that it is a serious situation.

QUEEN YOLANDA. Let me do penance for us both. Let me take the burden of his sin.

RAYMOND DE PENAFORTE. Only Christ may assume the sins of others. The King must repent.

QUEEN YOLANDA. He will. I promise you he will.

RAYMOND DE PENAFORTE. It is only through my intercession with Pope Urban that we have prevented the King's excommunication.

QUEEN YOLANDA. For which you have my undying thanks. (PAUSE) Will he recover?

RAYMOND DE PENAFORTE. Yes, the Bishop of Gerona will recover, thank God.

QUEEN YOLANDA. Thank God indeed. If I had been able to satisfy the King ... I've been replaced. He's smitten with her. I have less and less influence.

RAYMOND DE PENAFORTE. If you love your king as I know you do, you must use all your resources to strengthen his faith in Christ. For, it is not only the King's infidelity and the mutilation of the Bishop that concerns his Holiness. It is the favouring of the Jews.

QUEEN YOLANDA. Yes, the Jews. James is vulnerable now. He will need our help. He knows he has greatly offended all Christians.

RAYMOND DE PENAFORTE. The Pope requires a more active role. A serious effort by his Majesty to convert the Jews to Christianity. (PAUSE) Perhaps a Disputation.

QUEEN YOLANDA (INTRIGUED). That would be difficult. He was appalled by the disturbances in Paris.

RAYMOND DE PENAFORTE. Rome demands action.

QUEEN YOLANDA. Go to him. The King has always had respect for you. He will listen. I know he will accept Christianity into his heart when he finally understands as we do. He knows he has sinned.

RAYMOND DE PENAFORTE.(BOWING). You have great fervour.

SCENE TWO

KING JAMES, RAYMOND DE PENAFORTE, ALCONSTANTINI, ATTENDANT.

ENTER KING JAMES WITH BROADSWORD, FOLLOWED BY ATTENDANT.

KING JAMES. Did you see it? Two at once! That was broadswording. Their ages added together would not equal mine. Do you think they took it easy on me?

ALCONSTANTINI. They wouldn't dare, your Majesty.

KING JAMES. True, quite true. All right, begin, Raymond.

RAYMOND DE PENAFORTE. There seems to be some shortfall in the taxes due from the Jewish community of Barcelona.

KING JAMES. Look into the matter, then.

RAYMOND DE PENAFORTE. Perhaps, Don Alconstantini would be better placed to pursue this matter.

KING JAMES. Don Alconstantini is probably better placed to pursue most matters.

RAYMOND DE PENAFORTE. (ANNOYED) I cannot accept that, your Majesty. But this particular matter might be quite appropriate. Being a Jew himself, he may be better able to discover the source of the shortfall.

ALCONSTANTINI. Or to judge whether the Jews have in fact been wrongly accused of not paying the due amount.

KING JAMES. Don't bicker, you two. All right, Alconstantini, you look into the matter immediately. Next?

RAYMOND DE PENAFORTE. Don Oliver Napolitano and Don José Ruiz, accused of murder and treason, have admitted it was their intent to overthrow you. They await punishment.

KING JAMES. Stone them to death. Burn them in the town square. I should torture them, but I am a civilized man. Behead them.

RAYMOND DE PENAFORTE. No torture?

KING JAMES. No.

RAYMOND DE PENAFORTE. They still have not given us all the details of their plot.

KING JAMES. No. No torture. After all, they are noblemen.

RAYMOND DE PENAFORTE. King Louis of France requests your help in preventing escaped Jews from hiding in your Kingdom of Aragon.

KING JAMES. Why are they running?

RAYMOND DE PENAFORTE. They have been converted by force to Christianity and then returned to Judaism. Unfortunately, it is severely punishable in France.

KING JAMES. Send him a letter. Tell him that as always he may depend on my full cooperation in this matter, and may trust that I will continue my vigilance in dealing with the Jewish problem, however it presents itself. Solicitations, etc., etc. That should hold him. Are we done?

ATTENDANT. The Queen has returned from religious retreat.

KING JAMES. Oh, God, quickly, my back!

KING JAMES DOUBLES OVER IN PAIN. THE ATTENDANT BANGS ON THE KING'S BACK.

KING JAMES. Lower, lower! Harder, man, harder! Oh, God, yes, that's good, good. Oh, what I wouldn't do to be free of that pain!

RAYMOND DE PENAFORTE. One thing more, your Majesty.

RAYMOND SHOWS BOX.

KING JAMES (admiring box). Nice, eh? The finest ebony wood from Majorca. (Opens box) My, my, the Bishop had a long tongue. Display it in the town square.

RAYMOND DE PENAFORTE. Your Majesty, I must speak openly.

KING JAMES. Please do.

RAYMOND DE PENAFORTE. Pope Urban is outraged.

KING JAMES. The Bishop of Gerona brought it upon himself. He should not have spoken openly against his King.

RAYMOND DE PENAFORTE. He spoke against your infidelities.

KING JAMES. Well he's a mute bishop now, isn't he?

RAYMOND DE PENAFORTE. His Holiness feels that the incident is further proof of your lack of support for the Church. He has recommended excommunication.

KING JAMES. That would not be good.

RAYMOND DE PENAFORTE. I have been able to delay this while we seek calm. I do think that if the Pope felt that you had more of an interest in converting the Jews to Christianity, so that our Saviour may return, he would be willing to re-examine the penalty.

KING JAMES.   If Christ won't come until the Jews have been converted, then he just won't come.

RAYMOND DE PENAFORTE.   Your Majesty, that Christ will come again is a fundamental doctrine of the true faith, to doubt which could plunge a soul into everlasting hell.

KING JAMES.   Well, of course, I didn't quite mean that, Raymond. I know very well that Christ will come again. But if we have to convert the Jews first ...

RAYMOND DE PENAFORTE.   Holy writ assures us that that the Jews will be converted.

KING JAMES.   I know the Jews will be converted, Raymond. But the question is will they be converted by human means or divine means? I know the Jews better than you do. They are my scribes, my doctors, my attendants, and I say it will take a miracle to convert them to Christianity. They're damn sure of themselves. And they don't believe in hell. How can you convert them if they're not afraid of hell?

RAYMOND DE PENAFORTE.   I fear, your Majesty, that your long acquaintance with and over-reliance on the Jews has clouded your views on them. I hope to be the means, under God, of weaning you away from their influence. His Holiness is pleased to hear that the number of Jews among your courtiers has somewhat diminished lately.

KING JAMES.   Yes, but I can't get rid of them altogether. Who else is going to look after my affairs?

RAYMOND DE PENAFORTE.   Your very own Spanish noblemen.

KING JAMES.   That's a bad joke. My noblemen are rotten organisers except when they are organising against me. It's too bad we are no longer at war with the Moors. That kept the bastards busy. Now I have to watch them like a hawk.

RAYMOND DE PENAFORTE.   All the more reason to have the Pope on your side. The noblemen would be no match against you and the Church. We have sources of information about impending dangers that could be invaluable to you.

KING JAMES. My, my, my, you're as clever as a Jew, Raymond. Must be all that Hebrew you are studying.

RAYMOND DE PENAFORTE. Your Majesty knows that I promote the study of Hebrew in order to further my goal of converting the Jews to Christianity. Unbelief must be fought with its own weapons. It is no longer enough to make your townships abandon their Jewish advisers; you must yourself comply.

KING JAMES. Raymond, you must understand that my Jewish advisers are essential to my material affairs. As are all Jews. They are very good advisers, very eager to please, except in religious matters, of course. It is true that they are only a small percentage of the population, but they pay sixty percent of the taxes. I appreciate that. It would be hard to give them up.

RAYMOND DE PENAFORTE. If your spiritual affairs are in good order, a little disorder in the material affairs of your kingdom can soon be corrected. His Holiness is prepared to help with financial matters. You do not need the Jews anymore. The Church will advise you in matters both spiritual and temporal. If you look to the Christian in you...

KING JAMES. I am still very far from being a good Christian. I am lucky to have you as my confessor to help me towards repentance. (PAUSE) Raymond, do you really think that I am not too late to escape hellfire?

RAYMOND DE PENAFORTE. As long as you fear hell you have a chance of escaping it. The sufferings of Christ atone for all repentant sinners.

KING JAMES. However late they repent?

RAYMOND DE PENAFORTE. If you truly seek redemption, you will be accepted.

KING JAMES. I wish I could believe it. I can't convince myself that I am a genuine penitent. If a breath of youth and well-being blew through me, I'd be back to sinning. I am nothing but an old fraud thinking of creeping into heaven at the last while clinging to my lovely sins until the last possible moment.

RAYMOND DE PENAFORTE. God sends us old age and ill health in His great mercy, so that with a broken heart we may seek His grace.

KING JAMES. Then He is very merciful to me. I am a mass of ailments from head to foot. Brother Raymond, I can not give up my Jewish doctors.

RAYMOND DE PENAFORTE. Think of your spiritual good, my Lord. Has not the Pope forbidden all Christians to resort to these Jewish doctors?

KING JAMES. If you succeeded in converting all the Jews to Christianity, then could I keep my Jewish doctor? Or do Jews, on being converted, become bad doctors?
(THE KING HAS A LAUGH)
Yes. All right, as you say, let's speak openly. What does Rome want?

RAYMOND DE PENAFORTE. First, that you must remove all your Jewish consultants, advisers, administrators and doctors. Then, you must seek absolution for the Bishop of Gerona incident. In return the Pope, in his appreciation, will support you in your struggle with hostile noblemen. And His Holiness may also be willing to reduce your excommunication to an admonition.

KING JAMES. Oral or written?

RAYMOND DE PENAFORTE. Oral. Nothing written.

KING JAMES. Anything else?

RAYMOND DE PENAFORTE. I ask that your Majesty examine the pain you are causing your wife. She is overwrought.

THE KING IS SILENT.

RAYMOND DE PENAFORTE. Pope Urban would also like a Disputation to take place.

KING JAMES. A Disputation? No, no, they never work. Look what happened in Paris. Very few conversions and too many people died.

RAYMOND DE PENAFORTE. I believe that previous Disputations have been mismanaged, your Majesty.

KING JAMES. How so?

RAYMOND DE PENAFORTE. The chief mistake has been that we have attempted to dispute with the Jews without sufficient knowledge of the Jewish mind. The Jews cannot be driven by force into the kingdom of Christ. They must be persuaded by their very Jewishness.

KING JAMES. And how would you do that? (SOUND OF LATIN PRAYER)

RAYMOND DE PENAFORTE. I would remind your Majesty that we have not been entirely unsuccessful already. We have converted some very learned Jews who are now ornaments of our academy. I refer particularly to our cherished Brother Pablo Christiani.

SCENE THREE

PABLO CHRISTIANI KNEELS IN PRAYER. IT IS HIS VOICE PRAYING IN LATIN.

RAYMOND DE PENAFORTE. If we were able to convert this man, who was steeped in Jewish thought and worship, there is no Jew whom we cannot convert. Indeed, Pablo Christiani is the key to the conversion of the Jews. It is he who would be the representative of Christianity in a Disputation.

KING JAMES. What? Not yourself?

RAYMOND DE PENAFORTE. Certainly not myself. The Jews would see me as an antagonist. That would be a fatal mistake.

KING JAMES. I see. Let the former Jew dispute with the Jew. Very clever, Raymond.

RAYMOND DE PENAFORTE. I am honoured, your Majesty. But, do not overestimate me. I am simply sensible enough to realize that if I led the disputation myself it would have no chance of success. They must be led to Christ by one of their own; and by their own holy writings, which, when properly understood, confirm the truth of our religion. They must be persuaded by the treasures already in their possession, the Old Testament, and the Talmud.

LIGHTS FADE. ON PABLO CHRISTIANI STILL LOST IN FERVENT PRAYER.

KING JAMES. But, have we not often been told by learned and holy men that the Talmud is an abominable book, filled with blasphemies and devilry?

RAYMOND DE PENAFORTE. That is an accusation arising from ignorance. The Talmud is partly a great and holy work and, like the Old Testament, testifies to the incarnation of Christ. Previous Disputations have failed because invariably the Talmud, which the Jews love and revere, has been denounced.
Now, for the first time, the Jews will be faced by one who knows the Talmud as well as themselves, and loves it as they do.

SILENCE.

KING JAMES. A good match. A sporting match. And this is what the Pope wants? I like it. Agreed.

RAYMOND DE PENAFORTE. Very good your Majesty!

AS RAYMOND GOES TO EXIT, CONSUELO ENTERS FROM ANOTHER PLACE SPEAKING AS SHE ENTERS

CONSUELO. Has he gone?

RAYMOND TURNS BACK AND SEES HER.

RAYMOND DE PENAFORTE. Pablo Christiani will gather the remnant Israel into the hands of the Mother Church, and Christ Messiah will descend upon the earth and bless his great servant, King James the Conqueror, by whose wisdom and virtue the Disputation came about!

KING JAMES. And all my sins will be forgiven.

EXIT RAYMOND DE PENAFORTE.

CONSUELO. I don't trust that man. He's trying to get rid of me.

KING JAMES. What do you expect? He's a holy man, isn't he?

CONSUELO. You look tired. Come, let me rub you.

KING JAMES. You will have to go away. At least for the disputation.

CONSUELO. I won't go. You will need me.

CONSUELO RUBS THE KING'S SHOULDERS. SHE KISSES HIM. HE RESPONDS WITH PASSION. AFTER A MOMENT THE KING BREAKS FROM CONSUELO.

CONSUELO. What is it?

KING JAMES. Doesn't it bother you what we do?

CONSUELO. No

KING JAMES. It scares me.

CONSUELO. The conqueror of the Moors, afraid?

KING JAMES. I was never afraid of war. I am afraid of hell.

CONSUELO. That's what the church is for. What use are all these Bishops and priests, and confessors if they can't save us from hell? If we had no Church to save us, could we still do this?

SHE KISSES HIM.

KING JAMES. Is that why we are trying to convert the Jews? To make them into sinful Christians?

CONSUELO. The Jews will never be converted.

KING JAMES. What makes you so sure?

CONSUELO. There have to be Jews. They're part of the world. Like the devil. You couldn't convert the devil, could you?

KING JAMES. Perhaps.

CONSUELO. That would put the Pope and all the priests out of a job. There can be no world without the Devil - no sin, no confession. You may dispute all you wish.

JAMES. You think it's a waste of time, don't you?

CONSUELO. Not really. It will be fun to watch them trying to convert the Jews. Better than a circus. But it's a mistake, James. You won't get the better of them. They're too tricky. They are very learned in the secrets of magic! There's nothing they cannot do!

KING JAMES. You are a silly, superstitious woman. The Jews are only ordinary human beings who happen to be wrong about certain points of theology, on which we intend to put them right.

CONSUELO. They murdered Christ. That wasn't theology. That is what put them into the Kingdom of Satan and gave them their magic powers! That's why they can do things!

KING JAMES. Then we must rescue them from the power of the devil.

CONSUELO. That will upset the balance!

KING JAMES. What are you talking about?

CONSUELO. We Christians are saved from hell only by our beloved Jesus, is that right?

KING JAMES. Yes...

CONSUELO. If He had not been crucified none of us could be saved, do you agree?

KING JAMES. Yes...

CONSUELO. Well, who killed Jesus? The Jews. Don't you see? If all the Jews become Christians who will crucify Jesus for us?

SILENCE.

KING JAMES. You're an original theologian. Still, we must try to convert the Jews so that Christ may come again and the Day Of Judgment can occur.

CONSUELO. Why?

KING JAMES. The Second Coming of Christ? Doesn't every Christian want that?

CONSUELO. I don't. Not if there's a Day of Judgment along with it. I prefer things as they are. Christ saves us and the Jews take off our burden by being so much more wicked than us. Suppose we convert the Jews, they become Christians, and Christ does return? He will judge us all equally, the Jews as well. How do we know how He will judge? The Jews are our safeguard. They are like a tree in a thunderstorm that draws off lightning.

KING JAMES. Clever girl. But the Pope will have his Disputation. The Second Coming must be a good thing. At any event it is bound to be good for me.

CONSUELO. Perhaps not so good for me. The Disputation could be dangerous for anyone who does not look enough like a Christian. I heard that during the Paris Disputation ...

KING JAMES. The French are animals. I will have a civilized disputation. There will be no violence. (TAKING HER IN HIS ARMS) And I will kill the first one who breaks that law.

AN ATTENDANT ENTERS.

SCENE FOUR

ATTENDANT. The Queen.

CONSUELO disappears.

ENTER QUEEN YOLANDA.

QUEEN YOLANDA. You have done well, James.

KING JAMES. A word of praise from my queen?

QUEEN YOLANDA. Now you will be remembered as a great king. A great Catholic king!

KING JAMES. And not as a Jew-loving whore-monger?

QUEEN YOLANDA. Your whore-mongering I leave to your conscience and your confessor. As for your love of the Jews, you are now showing real love for them by trying to save their souls instead of making use of their suspect talents. Think of the happiness you will be bringing them by causing them to enter the Kingdom of Heaven!

KING JAMES. And suppose the Jews are not converted by the Disputation?

QUEEN YOLANDA. Pablo Christiani knows the Talmud well. He will convert the Rabbi and the rest will follow.

KING JAMES. What Rabbi?

QUEEN YOLANDA. There is a Rabbi whom they revere especially.

LIGHTS UP ON RABBI PRAYING.

KING JAMES. I didn't think the Jews revered anyone much.

QUEEN YOLANDA. It is true in general Jews have little sense of reverence. Reverence is a Christian virtue. Yet, there appears sometimes among them someone whom they admire; then their devotion is great. Such a man exists now.

KING JAMES. Who is he?

QUEEN YOLANDA. Rabbi Moses ben Nachman.

QUEEN YOLANDA. If he is converted, all the Jews will convert. We are convinced that Rabbi Moses is the key.

KING JAMES. (AS LIGHTS FADE ON RABBI) We? Who is we? You seem to know as much about the Jews as Raymond.

QUEEN YOLANDA. We must know as much as we can if we are to convert them. (PAUSE) James, you must grasp the importance of this sacred mission. God has called upon you to cleanse Aragon of all non-believers. And after Aragon, all of Spain.

KING JAMES. I am too old to conquer all of Spain.

QUEEN YOLANDA. If the Rabbi is converted you will not have to shoot one arrow

QUEEN YOLANDA TAKES JAMES' HAND AND DRAWS CLOSE. HE IS COLD TO HER BUT DOES NOT WITHDRAW HIS HAND.

KING JAMES. You are a very serious woman.

QUEEN YOLANDA.   It took you long to realize it.

QUEEN YOLANDA SENSUALLY KISSES HER HUSBAND'S HAND. HE WITHDRAWS IT.

KING JAMES.   I've always realized it. But men do not always want a serious woman. (PAUSE) What if you fail to convert the Rabbi?

QUEEN YOLANDA.   Then we must resort to other means.

KING JAMES.   Your love for the Jews is indeed great.

EXIT QUEEN YOLANDA.

SCENE FIVE

THE HOME OF MOSES BEN NACHMAN. MOSES READS AT A TABLE. ENTER JUDITH

JUDITH.   Father, there's a boy outside.

MOSES BEN NACHMAN.   Is he ill?

JUDITH.   He's not here to see you as a doctor. He says he's wanted by the Inquisition.

MOSES BEN NACHMAN.   Where has he come from?

JUDITH.   He's escaped from France. I told him we'd help to get him to a country where he could be a Jew without fear. A non-Christian country - Morocco, or better still, the Holy Land.

KNOCKING ON THE DOOR.

THEY FREEZE. MOSES NODS TO JUDITH. SHE OPENS THE DOOR. ENTER DON ALCONSTANTINI. HE BOWS TO JUDITH. SHE LIGHTLY BOWS. THERE IS SEXUAL TENSION BETWEEN THEM.

DON ALCONSTANTINI.   I must speak with you, Rabbi. (GIVES KING'S ORDER TO RABBI.)

MOSES BEN NACHMAN.   Ah, Don Alconstantini, so good of you to spare the time from your busy affairs. (RABBI READS ORDER.)

ALCONSTANTINI. The convert Pablo Christiani has been chosen to be your adversary. I realize we have had our differences in the past, Rabbi, but this Disputation makes it essential for us to act together.

MOSES BEN NACHMAN. I shall be happy to cooperate with you if I can.

RABBI GIVES KING'S ORDER TO JUDITH TO READ

ALCONSTANTINI. Many of us believe that now is the time to establish a base of power among the Jews. Always we delay at the request of the Rabbis. We wait until something like this Disputation to wake us up. I have offered to lead the community before, Rabbi. We must organize ourselves better.

MOSES BEN NACHMAN. Our unity is in our religion, not in giving power to one prominent individual or family. Not even the Alconstantinis.

ALCONSTANTINI. Our family is descended from the House of David.

MOSES BEN NACHMAN. All Israelites are the sons of kings; so said Rabbi Akiva.

ALCONSTANTINI. This King always kept his own counsel. But now it seems as if he is looking for sainthood, and we know what that will mean for the Jews.

JUDITH. Confiscation, expulsions and violence directed towards us.

ALCONSTANTINI. An end to all Jewish prosperity. This Disputation could affect me seriously. We Jewish landowners and merchants depend on the good will of the Monarch. All the good we are able to do for our fellow Jews depends on that. We must adopt a very cautious policy.

MOSES BEN NACHMAN. I understand. I do not wish to debate with the Christians for the very reasons you have stated. But we are in the hands of God. I have received orders from the King to attend.

ALCONSTANTINI. There may be an opportunity to avoid the entire issue. My friends are working on the matter. A word here, a word there. A favor done, a favor promised. I myself, in my position at Court, have the ear of the King, and may be able to put in a useful word.

MOSES BEN NACHMAN.   I hope your efforts are successful.

ALCONSTANTINI.   If I am not successful and you must dispute, the main thing is to say nothing offensive.

MOSES BEN NACHMAN.   That will be not be an easy thing to do.

ALCONSTANTINI.   Keep away from controversial matters. Confine yourself to defending Judaism from charges of blasphemy. Do not refer to Christianity as a false religion. They have their religion and we have ours, and the less we comment on theirs the better.

MOSES BEN NACHMAN.   If I am forced to speak it will do little justice to Judaism to say nothing memorable about it.

ALCONSTANTINI.   Think of the danger if you do.

MOSES BEN NACHMAN.   Think of the danger if I don't.

ALCONSTANTINI.   You have a great responsibility to all Jews. Don't be a martyr and don't make martyrs of the rest of us.

MOSES BEN NACHMAN.   I will do nothing foolish. I must judge by what I find.

ALCONSTANTINI.   Perhaps you should consider going away.

MOSES BEN NACHMAN.   No. The Disputation will take place whether I am here or not.

ALCONSTANTINI.   Perhaps someone else could take your place.

JUDITH.   No one can replace my father. No one can replace Moses ben Nachman.

MOSES BEN NACHMAN.   See, a good daughter.

ALCONSTANTINI.   What does it matter who is there? Do you think Raymond de Penaforte or Pablo Christiani will take any notice of what you say? If someone less learned or less ready-tongued takes your place, will it make any difference? In any event they will place restrictions on what you are allowed to say. They are hoping to convert you and when you refuse...

MOSES BEN NACHMAN. The King demands my presence. We are in God's hands. Thank you, Don Alconstantini, for your concern.

EXIT MOSES BEN NACHMAN.

ALCONSTANTINI. This isn't one of his debates with Rabbi Jonah, or Rabbi Zerachia.

JUDITH. Those could be pretty fierce, too.

ALCONSTANTINI. But those were wars of the Lord in which no blood is shed. This is different. He must be careful. Don't forget we all need him. Everyone is anxious.

JUDITH. He will know what to do. (PAUSE) Don Alconstantini, there is a boy waiting outside who is an escaped Jew from France. He needs help ...

ALCONSTANTINI. My God, no! I shouldn't be here! I cannot be concerned with this...my position at court..it is important that I be kept away from this kind of thing... (SUDDENLY ASHAMED) What is it you need?

JUDITH. Money.

ALCONSTANTINI. What?

JUDITH. For transportation and bribes. He has to leave the country.

ALCONSTANTINI. Yes. I only mean that I should not know too much.

ALCONSTANTI GOES INTO HIS MONEY POUCH. GIVES JUDITH SMALL BAG OF COINS.

JUDITH. Thank you. It is a good thing you have done.

ALCONSTANTINI. I am known everywhere for doing good things.

UNCOMFORTABLE PAUSE.

ALCONSTANTINI. Judith, I have a gift for you.

HE DISPLAYS A LARGE SWATCH OF RED SILK.

UNCOMFORTABLE PAUSE

ALCONSTANTINI. Silk, I have first choice as part of my monthly allotment.

JUDITH. I cannot accept this.

ALCONSTANTINI. Please. Just this once.

JUDITH. It would not be right.

ALCONSTANTINI. It would mean everything to me if you would take it.

JUDITH. It means too much, then.

ALCONSTANTINI. Why? You must tell me.

JUDITH. I am the daughter of a Rabbi and you are a courtier, a good thing to be sure, but we are scholars. We have been for generations. And I am expected to marry a scholar.

ALCONSTANTINI. Not all of us have leisure for scholarship. The community must be served. Moreover, I have helped many a scholar financially to pursue his studies, just as Zebulun helped Issachar. (JUDITH LOOKS UP RATHER STARTLED AT THIS DISPLAY OF LEARNING. ALCONSTANTINI NODS.) I have learned enough of the Talmud to know that to help a scholar is as meritorious as to be one. There is no law that commands you to marry a scholar.

JUDITH. Don Alconstantini, if I marry and when I marry I will marry a scholar.

A HURT ALCONSTANTINI BOWS HIS HEAD.

UNCOMFORTABLE PAUSE.

JUDITH. I must help the boy.

ALCONSTANTINI. (HIS HURT TURNING TO ANGER). You are further jeopardizing us by smuggling foreigners out of Spain.

JUDITH. They're Jews!

ALCONSTANTINI. They're French. They are not our problem.

JUDITH. But ...

ALCONSTANTINI. (OVERRIDING HER) They are wanted criminals from a foreign country whose King is our ally.

JUDITH. They are Jews and they will die without our help. You are only afraid of losing your wealth and position in the court. You pretend to care but you do not care!

ALCONSTANTINI. I am a leader among my people!

JUDITH. Your pretension to authority over Jews is nauseating! You look upon the commandments as mere customs. You scoff at the words of the Sages and you put the accumulation of wealth before your relationship with God.

ALCONSTANTINI IS SHOCKED YET MOVED BY JUDITH'S PASSION.

ALCONSTANTINI. I can see now that your contempt for me runs deep. You are young and you do not understand everything, and since you have your father's ear I recommend you emphasize caution in disputing with Christians. I also recommend you put aside your clandestine career. Everything that happens in this Kingdom is eventually known to the Dominicans. People are going to die soon if we are not careful. You may tell your father that.

EXIT ALCONSTANTINI. RE-ENTER MOSES.

JUDITH. Another visit from the great courtier.

MOSES BEN NACHMAN. He does what he can. He would deny you nothing.

JUDITH. Except myself. (PAUSE) Is he right? Is it really so dangerous?

MOSES BEN NACHMAN. It's hard to tell.

JUDITH. Perhaps you should go away ...

MOSES BEN NACHMAN. The king has commanded my presence. How can I refuse? Could I ask you to stop what you do?

JUDITH. No. (THEY LOOK AT EACH OTHER AND EMBRACE.)

MOSES BEN NACHMAN. We are in God's hands.

JUDITH. What a ridiculous thing this Disputation is! They are going to teach Rabbi Moses ben Nachman, the great Ramban, the meaning of our holy books! Moses ben Nachman is going to be told that he never understood our holy books, and if he did understand them, he'd become a Christian, God forbid! It's enough to make one laugh. And who is going to argue against him? Pablo Christiani, the apostate, who used to be a third-rate pupil of Rabbi Eliezer of Tarascon who listened to the words of our Rabbi as if he were at Mount Sinai. Pablo Christiani - if he learns for seven years, he might become an ignoramus. What is this madness?

MOSES BEN NACHMAN. The war with the Moors kept them busy. Now with no Moors to kill, they turn against us.

JUDITH. Yes, and now their warriors are the Dominicans. These friars are everywhere - Dominicans, Franciscans, they're all the same, though they hate each other.

MOSES BEN NACHMAN. All are united in the great cause of turning Jews into Christians.

JUDITH. " Why don't we become Christians?", they want to know. Is that why we crossed the Red Sea? " Don't we want to be saved?", they want to know. All I want to be saved from is the Dominicans.

MOSES HAS DONNED HIS PRAYER-SHAWL (TALLIT)

MOSES BEN NACHMAN. (PRAYING) Ashrei yoshevei veitecha, od yehallelucha, selah. (*"Happy are those who dwell in thy house; they shall praise thee continually."*)

MOSES MURMURS THE REST OF THE PRAYER AND BOWS IN SILENCE FOR THE AMIDAH PRAYER.

SCENE SIX

A CHRISTIAN SANCTUARY IN THE COURT OF KING JAMES.

RAYMOND DE PENAFORTE KNEELS ON A TWO-MAN PRIE-DIEUX.

ENTER BROTHER PABLO CHRISTIANI.

PABLO CHRISTIANI. Brother Raymond ...?

RAYMOND DE PENAFORTE. Oh, Brother Pablo. Forgive me.

PABLO CHRISTIANI. Not at all. Your thoughts range over all of Christendom and far beyond. A worldwide campaign for God is in progress. And you are its architect.

PABLO KNEELS NEXT TO RAYMOND AND MAKES THE SIGN OF THE CROSS.

RAYMOND DE PENAFORTE. If my plans become too grandiose I shall be grateful for any criticism you have to offer Brother Pablo.

PABLO CHRISTIANI. If I may?

RAYMOND DE PENAFORTE. Of course.

PABLO CHRISTIANI. Not too grandiose. But, perhaps a little too hopeful. You place great reliance on the power of reason. But, suppose the Jews are not, in the last resort, moved by reason?

RAYMOND DE PENAFORTE. Are you feeling doubtful about the disputation?

PABLO CHRISTIANI. No. I am prepared. I do think, though, that I have a somewhat different view of its purpose from yours.

RAYMOND DE PENAFORTE. In what way?

PABLO CHRISTIANI. I think of it more as a way of exerting pressure.

RAYMOND DE PENAFORTE. Surely reason itself is the greatest pressure.

PABLO CHRISTIANI. It depends on who is putting it forward.

RAYMOND DE PENAFORTE. Reason is reason.

PABLO CHRISTIANI. Good reasons are nothing unless they are backed by power.

RAYMOND DE PENAFORTE. Was it the power of the Church then, rather than its arguments, that turned you from Jew to Christian?

PABLO CHRISTIANI. Power itself is the best of arguments. (PAUSE) What was left of my family came here from France, fleeing the massacres. I have seen the horrible results when the Jews have resisted conversion. They must realize that they have been utterly defeated. God has given the power to the Christians. How long must the Jews go on suffering by swimming against the tide of history?

RAYMOND DE PENAFORTE. The French are barbaric. King Louis has said that the best way to dispute with a Jew is to drive a dagger into his heart.

PABLO CHRISTIANI. At least the Jews in France know where they stand with him. He makes them wear yellow badges to mark them out.

RAYMOND DE PENAFORTE. I understand you had a hand in that.

PABLO CHRISTIANI. It was my idea.

RAYMOND DE PENAFORTE. You are in Spain, now, Brother Pablo. There will be no undue pressures in this disputation. No threats. No bullying. Do you understand?

PABLO CHRISTIANI. Of course. We must proceed with caution. But, I do feel that in the long run it will be no kindness to the Jews to feed their illusions. God's favor has turned away from them. They will find peace only in the bosom of the Church.

RAYMOND DE PENAFORTE. By reason and reason alone. Is that understood?

PABLO BOWS HIS HEAD.

RAYMOND DE PENAFORTE. Your fervor is admirable, Brother Pablo. You will make a good Archbishop one day. But, you must keep more in mind the compassionate teachings of Jesus. Just think of what a wonderful Christian Rabbi Moses will make. (PAUSE) Tell me, Brother Pablo, do you ever miss being a Jew?

PABLO CHRISTIANI. Sometimes. When the festivals come around. Or I'll pass a synagogue and strains of music will reach me.

RAYMOND DE PENAFORTE. These feelings are quite natural.

PABLO CHRISTIANI. No. They must be suppressed. Their whole world is obsolete. God has pronounced judgment on it.

SCENE SEVEN

KING JAMES AND QUEEN YOLANDA. ATTENDANTS PREPARE THE ROOM FOR THE DISPUTATION. SPECTATORS ENTER THE COURT AND TAKE UP POSITIONS ON EITHER SIDE.

RAYMOND DE PENAFORTE. May I present to your Majesties Brother Pablo Christiani.

KING JAMES. I have heard much about you, Pablo.

PABLO CHRISTIANI. If I can be the humble means of the enlightenment of my erring nation I shall not have lived in vain.

KING JAMES. Tell me, Pablo, were you really once a rabbi?

PABLO CHRISTIANI. Not quite a rabbi, your Majesty, but one training to be a rabbi. Yet, I have always been oppressed by the feeling that the Jews were rejected by God. I had almost completed my training in the Talmud when the truth came upon me that certain obscure sayings in the Jewish Talmud testified to God's plan for fulfilling Judaism in Christianity. I searched further and further and every step confirmed my first insight. I hope fervently to lead my brothers along that same path.

QUEEN YOLANDA. It will be a blessed work.

ENTER AN ATTENDANT. HE WHISPERS INTO RAYMOND'S EAR.

KING JAMES. When you were a Jew, Pablo, were you trained as a physician? I have this lower back...

PABLO CHRISTIANI. No, your Majesty, I have had no training in that art.

RAYMOND DE PENAFORTE. Your Majesties, the Rabbi, Moses Ben Nachman, has arrived in obedience to your royal summons.

KING JAMES. Good, good, get him at once.

EXIT RAYMOND DE PENAFORTE

KING JAMES. You can meet your opponent, Brother Pablo.

PABLO CHRISTIANI. Your Majesty is most considerate.

KING JAMES. This promises to be a most interesting contest.

QUEEN YOLANDA. James, I would beg you to adopt a more serious attitude towards the Disputation. This is not a cockfight or a tournament between your knights.

KING JAMES. You are of course quite right, Yolanda. But, one cannot help taking a certain sporting interest.

ENTER RAYMOND DE PENAFORTE AND MOSES BEN NACHMAN.

RAYMOND DE PENAFORTE. May I present to your Majesties, Rabbi Moses ben Nachman.

KING JAMES. Rabbi Moses, I have heard a great deal about you. I know that you are a person well worthy of representing the Jewish community in our Disputation.

MOSES BEN NACHMAN. (BOWING) With all respect, your Majesty, it is an honor which I would much prefer to decline.

KING JAMES. Decline? I am disappointed in you, Rabbi. Does the opposition frighten you?

MOSES BEN NACHMAN. Not at all, your Majesty. I am not afraid of opposition. Nor am I averse to Disputations. I have been engaged in Disputations all my life.

QUEEN YOLANDA. Then what is your objection?

MOSES BEN NACHMAN. When the lion invites the mouse to a Disputation, the mouse, however fond he may be of arguing, will do well to avoid the invitation. For the poor mouse does not know what to fear most, losing the argument or winning it.

KING JAMES. What is it you fear?

MOSES BEN NACHMAN. There have been other Disputations, your Majesty, and they have always ended with suffering for the Jewish people. In Paris recently...

KING JAMES. Tut, tut, man. We are Spaniards here. The French are one thing, we are another. We know the rules of fair play. I guarantee your personal safety and that of your fellow Jews both during and after the Disputation.

MOSES BEN NACHMAN. I thank your Majesty and accept your assurances.

KING JAMES. Good. Let's begin.

MOSES BEN NACHMAN. There is one other point I do wish to raise, if I may. In the other Disputations many rules were laid down concerning what the Jewish disputants were allowed to say.

KING JAMES. I don't understand.

RAYMOND DE PENAFORTE. It was necessary to lay down some rules. Otherwise, the Jewish participants might have uttered some shocking blasphemies.

MOSES BEN NACHMAN. May I ask the learned Brother Raymond, your Majesty, whether he intends to lay down such rules for the present Disputation?

RAYMOND DE PENAFORTE. Very few, your Majesty. It is necessary to ensure that no blasphemy should be uttered against the person of our beloved Lord and Savior, or His Blessed Mother, the Virgin Mary.

MOSES BEN NACHMAN. I am afraid that if I am to represent the case for Judaism adequately, I cannot undertake to avoid remarks which to a Christian might appear blasphemous.

SILENCE.

KING JAMES. I agree. The Rabbi is right. He must not be shackled before the contest.

RAYMOND DE PENAFORTE. Your Majesty ...

KING JAMES. You have my permission to use any arguments you choose, Rabbi Moses. You have complete liberty of speech in the Disputation.

Christ, not by violence but by reasoning and persuasion. Speaking for Christianity is Brother Pablo Christiani. Speaking for Judaism, Rabbi Moses ben Nachman. Rabbi?

MOSES BEN NACHMAN. Your Majesties, I too believe reason is alone sufficient to settle these matters. .

KING JAMES NODS.

MOSES BEN NACHMAN. Of the many issues we may try to cover, I suggest that we devote ourselves to two questions, which, in my view are the most vital.

KING JAMES. And they are?

MOSES BEN NACHMAN. The first question is, "Has the Messiah come, or is He yet to come?". The second question is, "Is the Messiah prophesied in the Bible a man or a divine being?".

PABLO CHRISTIANI. Very well, I agree.

KING JAMES. I am astonished that we have reached agreement on the agenda so quickly.

PABLO CHRISTIANI. Your Majesty, there is one point I wish to emphasize. Rabbi Moses has referred to the prophecies in the Hebrew Scriptures. It is my contention the Talmud also proves that the Divine Messiah has come.

KING JAMES. Rabbi Moses, do you agree that the Talmud should be brought into our discussion?

MOSES BEN NACHMAN. I have no objection, your Majesty. However, I should like to give Brother Pablo a friendly warning which may save him a great deal of time and trouble.

KING JAMES. What's that?

MOSES BEN NACHMAN. Simply that we Jews do not always agree with everything we find in the Talmud.

KING JAMES. I don't understand. Do you not accept the Talmud as a holy book to Jews?

MOSES BEN NACHMAN. I do. But, the Talmud is a record of discussions. These discussions took place over the course of about five hundred years on every aspect of Jewish religion. Obviously when two rabbis disagree, which happens on every page of the Talmud, both cannot be accepted as right. Consequently many sayings in the Talmud are not accepted by the Jews.

KING JAMES. Hmph.

MOSES BEN NACHMAN. Moreover, your Majesty, there is another point to be considered. It is only the legal parts of the Talmud, the Halakhah, which Jews consider binding. The non-legal parts, the Haggadah, being poetical and open to various interpretations, are not considered binding. And the subject of the Messiah belongs to the poetical part of the Talmud.

KING JAMES. This is a very strange Holy book.

MOSES BEN NACHMAN. The Talmud is a Holy book. But, it is not what the Christians mean by a Holy book.

KING JAMES. What about the Bible? Do you not see the Bible as a Holy book? Even more than the Talmud?

MOSES BEN NACHMAN. Yes, it is. But then again we are seldom sure what the Bible means. That is what the discussions in the Talmud are all about.

KING JAMES. I think we should get this point clear before we continue. Brother Pablo, can you elicit from Rabbi Moses a clear statement as to which writings or sayings or pronouncements he regards as authoritative?

PABLO CHRISTIANI. I shall do my best, your Majesty. Now, Rabbi Moses, I think you have been overstating the flexibility of the Jewish religious attitude. I was a Jew myself for many years and your description of Judaism does not quite tally with my memory of it.

MOSES BEN NACHMAN. Perhaps you have forgotten some things since you have become a Christian.

PABLO CHRISTIANI. I do not think so.

MOSES BEN NACHMAN. Or perhaps there were certain things about Judaism that you never understood.

PABLO CHRISTIANI. Again, I don't think so. Tell me, Rabbi Moses, is there such a thing as heresy in the Jewish religion?

MOSES BEN NACHMAN. Yes.

PABLO CHRISTIANI. What is a heretic, then, in Jewish law?

MOSES BEN NACHMAN. A Jew who denies an essential principle of Jewish faith.

PABLO CHRISTIANI. And what are the essential principles of Jewish faith?

MOSES BEN NACHMAN. That is a matter of dispute.

LAUGHTER FROM THE GALLERY.

THE KING RAISES A HAND AND THE GALLERY QUIETS.

PABLO CHRISTIANI. Surely there are some articles of faith that are beyond dispute.

MOSES BEN NACHMAN. There are some. The unity of God is one. The Revelation on Mount Sinai is another. But, we have no agreed and definitive set of theological doctrines, as the Christians have, for which they are prepared to burn people as heretics.

AN UNEASINESS RIPPLES THROUGH THE ARENA.

PABLO CHRISTIANI. Is it not true, Rabbi Moses, that the Jews give great respect to the recorded sayings of the rabbis, even though they may not necessarily be fully authoritative?

MOSES BEN NACHMAN. That is so.

PABLO CHRISTIANI. Does that apply to every recorded saying in the Talmud?

MOSES BEN NACHMAN. Yes, to every saying by an accredited rabbi.

PABLO CHRISTIANI. If you found that many sayings of these accredited rabbis point to the conclusion that the Messiah has already come and that He is divine, would this fact impress you?

MOSES BEN NACHMAN. It certainly would.

PABLO CHRISTIANI. That will suffice. I propose to prove to you that many sayings in the Talmud show unmistakably both that the Messiah has come and that His nature is divine.

MOSES BEN NACHMAN. If you can prove that you will have struck a great blow for your side.

KING JAMES. Excellent! Let's begin.

RAYMOND DE PENAFORTE. The first question is, "Has the Messiah come, or is he yet to come?". Brother Pablo?

PABLO CHRISTIANI. Your Majesty, let me cite a passage not from the Old Testament but from the Talmud. The Talmud says, "At the time when the Temple was destroyed, the Messiah was born.". What an extraordinary statement. The Jewish Temple was destroyed about twelve hundred years ago, very near the time of the beginning of Christianity. Let me put the question directly to Rabbi Moses. Why are the Jews waiting for the Messiah when their own Talmud tells them that He came twelve hundred years ago?

APPRECIATIVE REACTION FROM THE GALLERY.

KING JAMES. What have you to say to this, Rabbi Moses?

MOSES BEN NACHMAN. Your Majesty, with respect to Brother Pablo, the Talmud does not say that the Messiah came at the time of the destruction of the Temple. It only says the He was born then.

KING JAMES. That's more or less the same, no?

MOSES BEN NACHMAN. No, your Majesty. When Moses was born he did not immediately lead the children of Israel out of Egypt. That was hardly a task for a new born babe. The event itself took place eighty years later. Similarly, the date of the Messiah's birth is by no means the same as the date of His coming.

KING JAMES. And when will be His coming?

MOSES BEN NACHMAN. When he leads the Jews back to the Holy Land. That hasn't happened yet so he hasn't yet come

PABLO CHRISTIANI. Do you mean to tell us that the Messiah was born twelve hundred years ago and he still hasn't come?

MOSES BEN NACHMAN. Yes.

KING JAMES. I'd like to know who his doctor is. ...

MOSES BEN NACHMAN. Well, your Majesty, Adam lived almost as long as that. And Elijah, who never died, has lived very much longer and will return together with the Messiah.

KING JAMES. Where has the Messiah been all this time, then?

MOSES BEN NACHMAN. The Talmud says in the Garden of Eden.

KING JAMES. If you can believe that you can believe anything.

MOSES BEN NACHMAN. Many more incredible things than that are believed in the name of religion, your Majesty.

THE IMPLICATION IS NOT LOST ON THE SPECTATORS.

MOSES BEN NACHMAN. I personally do not believe that the Messiah was born at the time of the destruction of the Temple, I believe that He has not yet been born.

PABLO CHRISTIANI. But, the Talmud says quite distinctly that He was born then.

MOSES BEN NACHMAN. It is poetry. A parable. Certainly parables are not hard for a Christian to understand. It is a way of saying that hope is born in the very depths of despair. It should not be taken literally.

PABLO CHRISTIANI. Are you saying that the Talmud is lying?

MOSES BEN NACHMAN. A parable is not a lie.

PABLO CHRISTIANI. It is clear that the Rabbi is shifting his ground.

MOSES BEN NACHMAN. Not at all. If you want to take it literally that the Messiah was born at the time of the destruction of the Temple then you have my answer. Personally, I do not take it literally. I do not think He was born then or has been born since. Surely that is clear.

PABLO CHRISTIANI. What is clear to me is that your own Holy Book states that the Messiah has already come. But I shall offer you stronger proof of it. This argument depends not on the interpretation of texts, but on the great course of history. God reveals Himself in the texts of Scripture and in inspired traditions; this we can all agree on. But, He reveals Himself even more surely in history, for what happens must be by His will. History shall be my proof. Once the Jews were a mighty nation, with a Temple in Jerusalem which was the wonder of the world. God decided that the Temple should be razed to the ground, and instead the Christian Church should arise with its center in Rome and its great cathedrals in many lands, each outshining that Temple at the height of its glory. God made that decision. It was His will! And what of the Jews? They have become slaves and exiles. Is not this the strongest proof that they have lost, and the Church has won? The Messiah has come and the Christian Church is the living proof. Let the Jews cease to fight against the truth of history. Instead of dragging out a miserable existence that can only become more and more wretched as time goes on, let them join in the triumph of the Church! The Jews turned their faces against the Messiah when He came and now God turns His face against them. I know. I was a Jew. I suffered under that curse! But, Jesus Christ released me! He can release anyone who comes to Him. God's Church is merciful. The door is still open. Let the Jews enter and share in God's manifold blessings. Before it is too late!

THE GALLERY EXPLODES. THEY BEGIN A ROUSING CHANT. THE KING LETS THEM GO ON. THEY EVENTUALLY GROW SILENT, AWAITING THE RABBI'S REPLY.

MOSES BEN NACHMAN. Your Majesty, I must say at once that Brother Pablo's arguments have left me entirely unconvinced. That the Messiah has come, says the good Brother, is proved by the triumph of the Church. I would assume that means that we are now living in the Messianic era prophesied in the Bible. Glory was prophesied and glory is here in the shape of the Pope and priesthood and cathedrals and mighty rulers. So says Brother Pablo. But, is this indeed the Messianic era? When we read from the Bible in the prophecies of Ezekiel and Zechariah about the coming of the Messiah, what is the obvious thing that strikes us? It is that the coming of the Messiah will make the world a different place. Instead of a world of strife and bloodshed, of ceaseless agony and famine and warfare, there will be a world of peace and good will, a time of Sabbath, when swords are beaten into ploughshares, and the wolf will lie down with the lamb, and the peace of God will reach into the four corners of the earth. This is the time of the Messiah to which we Jews look forward, when the apparently meaningless agonies of the past will all prove to have had meaning after all, and true history will begin; when our struggles will prove to have been the birth-pangs of a better world. But, what has happened? Over twelve hundred years after the birth of Jesus I look around the world. Is this a world of peace? Have the swords been beaten into ploughshares? No. The world is more full of war than ever, and the most warlike of peoples, a people whose fierceness is greater than that of wolves, are the people of Christendom!

THE GALLERY VOICES HEAVY DISAPPROVAL.

PABLO CHRISTIANI. He blasphemes!

KING JAMES. Silence!

COMPLETE SILENCE.

MOSES BEN NACHMAN. With all respect, your Majesty, you are a great king in Christendom. Your knights in armor clash like thunder. You have your foot soldiers and archers and your engines of war. If you believe that the Messiah has come why do you not dismiss all your soldiers and enter the peace of God? Because the world is full of war and armies. Not far away is the army of the Moslems, and beyond them the army of the Mongols and the Tartars, and beyond them who knows what other armies? Where does it say in the writings of our Prophets, which you say you believe, that the Messiah would bring not love but hate, not peace but war? The time of the Messiah was to be a time of justice. I look around the world which you Christians have made out of your faith in Jesus. Is it a world of justice? It seems in the Christian world everybody lords over somebody. Yet, there is no Jewish aristocracy, no Jewish slavery. No Jew is lord over Jews. No other nation in the world has learned to live this way. I ask you, have you a higher standard to teach us? What has happened to the "new heart" Ezekiel spoke of when he said, "I will give you a heart of flesh instead of a heart of stone."? If this is the new world of which the Prophets spoke, it would have been better if they had remained silent!

RAYMOND DE PENAFORTE. Your Majesty, I must speak! We Christians are never nearer to Christ that when we suffer from oppression, as Christ Himself suffered! A slave can come to Christ as well as or better that an emperor.

MOSES BEN NACHMAN. That is a very comfortable doctrine for oppressors to hear. I don't believe that anyone is better for being a slave.

RAYMOND DE PENAFORTE. Freedom and equality must wait until the Second Coming.

MOSES BEN NACHMAN. It seems all the real benefits of the coming of the Messiah are left for the Second Coming.

RAYMOND DE PENAFORTE. The First Coming has not been without its benefits.

MOSES BEN NACHMAN. Ah, yes, the triumph of the Church. Brother Pablo has made a great point of this. And the failure of the Jews, and our suffering. Christians make a great mystery of failure. They talk of their suffering Messiah whose failure proves his divinity. And in the same breath they say that the Jews' failure and suffering proves they are accursed. The sufferings of the Jews were predicted by the Hebrew Prophets, who also predicted that a time would come when the nations of the world would acknowledge that the Jews have suffered for the sins of the world!

RAYMOND DE PENAFORTE. It is Christ who suffered for the sins of the world, not the Jews! And so it was foretold by the prophet Isaiah!

MOSES BEN NACHMAN. And I say that the Suffering Servant depicted in Isaiah was not Jesus but the Jewish people, and that the Suffering Servant is still in your midst, and you followers of Jesus are his chief persecutors!
OUTRAGE AND CONFUSION FROM THE GALLERY.

PABLO CHRISTIANI. Your Majesty, are we to allow such blasphemy?! He is saying that the Jews are Christ and we Christians are his crucifiers!

THE CROWD EXPLODES IN ANGER.

KING JAMES OVERRIDES THEM.

KING JAMES. I promised him free speech.

AN UNCOMFORTABLE MURMURING GROWS IN THE GALLERY.

MOSES BEN NACHMAN.   We have only to look around the world to see that the Messiah has not come. A Messiah who does not make the world better is no Messiah. And a Messiah who tells us it does not matter whether the world is better is worse than no Messiah! We Jews say that the world is still unredeemed. The Messiah has not come. And the Messiah will not come until the world has deserved to receive Him!

BLACKOUT.

ACT TWO

SCENE ONE

QUEEN YOLANDA AND PABLO CHRISTIANI.

QUEEN YOLANDA. The Rabbi is a fiend! Satan speaks from his mouth! Only the devil himself could have such cunning. I have heard that he is a master of their black magic, the Kabbalah.

PABLO CHRISTIANI. The Rabbi is an expert Kabbalist, but the Kabbalah is not black magic. It is simply a mystical philosophy. It in no way invokes the devil.

QUEEN YOLANDA. Tell me the truth, when you were a Jew, did you never see black magic practised? Did you never see Christian children sacrificed and their blood used for unholy purposes?

PABLO CHRISTIANI. Your Majesty, such practices are unheard of among the Jews. They are not an uncivilized people. If anything, they are over-civilized. They think they are too clever to need salvation.

QUEEN YOLANDA. I see little sign of his breaking down. Are we to allow his insults to Christ to go unpunished?

PABLO CHRISTIANI. The king has ruled. The Rabbi will continue to speak freely.

QUEEN YOLANDA. If I had my way I'd have him broken on the wheel and burnt.

PABLO CHRISTIANI. It is clear we are unlikely to convert the Rabbi or bring about a mass conversion. This event, as I see it, is the beginning of a long campaign.

QUEEN YOLANDA. Campaign?

PABLO CHRISTIANI. They must be made to understand that the atmosphere has changed in Aragon. When the Disputation is completed, let me flood the countryside with accounts of the event, demonstrating the defeat of the Jewish argument. Then I will address the Jewish congregations calling for conversions.

QUEEN YOLANDA. The Rabbi is no fool. He will write his own account.

PABLO CHRISTIANI. If he does he has sealed his fate. The king gave him permission to speak, not to write. If he writes down blasphemies such as he has spoken, his blood will be upon his own head.

QUEEN YOLANDA. James may take a different view

PABLO CHRISTIANI. Then it would be a matter for Papal intervention. The King cannot afford to cross the Pope.

QUEEN YOLANDA. The King's position must not be weakened.

PABLO CHRISTIANI. Of course not.

QUEEN YOLANDA. God bless you, Pablo. You have given me new heart.

SCENE TWO

MOSES BEN NACHMAN'S LODGINGS. MOSES BEN NACHMAN AND JUDITH.

ENTER DON ALCONSTANTINI.

MOSES. Peace to you, Don Alconstantini!

ALCONSTANTINI. Peace? What peace? We have a dangerous situation now. It is time to curb your tongue, Rabbi. It is time to try conciliation.

JUDITH. My father spoke like an angel.

ALCONSTANTINI. Let us hope that it was not the angel of death.

JUDITH. Did you not admire his words? Did you not forget, at least for a moment, that we are a helpless people?

ALCONSTANTINI. Helpless, yes. Now we are back to reality. Everyone is hiding. Afraid to go anywhere. To work. To market. The Dominicans and the Queen are furious. They began the Disputation in quite a generous mood. All you had to do was to be polite, make it clear that you are not prepared to convert, yes, and refrain from attacking their religion. Then they might have let the matter rest, but now they are in a mood for all kinds of mischief.

JUDITH. My father must consider the long term effects.

ALCONSTANTINI. And what of the short term?

MOSES BEN NACHMAN. Let it not be said of us in this generation that we remained silent out of fear. We must send a message to future generations.

ALCONSTANTINI. We must take good care to ensure that there will be some future generations. You are being naive, Rabbi. This is not just a matter of religion. It is a matter of high politics. There are considerations here that you know nothing of. The King is not so secure on his throne as you think. (PAUSE) And there is another matter. I have heard that after the Disputation is over, the Dominicans will seek some pretext to demand your death. It is only a rumour, but I have heard it from many quarters.

MOSES BEN NACHMAN. I thank you, Don Alconstantini, for your advice. I understand our shared responsibility for the safety of our people. I shall give good weight to your counsel.

ALCONSTANTINI. Thank you. That is all I ask. Some calm is all I ask. Judith, I am sorry for my past rudeness. Forgive me. This has been a difficult time. I am ... I don't know ... Here. In case. You know ...

GIVES HER A SMALL BAG OF COINS.

JUDITH. (SOFTENING) Thank you, Don Alconstantini.

ALCONSTANTINI. You're welcome. You know I would do anything for our people.

EXIT ALCONSTANTINI.

JUDITH. Is he right?

MOSES BEN NACHMAN. After the Disputation is over, the Dominicans may well ask for my death. And there may be some pressure to curtail Jewish privileges generally. We are far better off in Aragon than in other Christian countries. But this Disputation may change everything. The King is still my best hope. I pray that I may be the only one to suffer. For myself (HE SHRUGS) ... but what will become of you? Alconstantini would take care of you.

JUDITH. Yes, he would take care of me; and I would be obliged to a man who would do anything to maintain his position. How long do you think it would take, Father, for Don Alconstantini to become a Christian?

MOSES BEN NACHMAN IS SILENT.

SCENE THREE

KING JAMES AND CONSUELO.

CONSUELO. I told you the Rabbi would be too tricky.

KING JAMES. He certainly seems to have a damnably clever answer to everything Pablo and Raymond throw at him.

CONSUELO. I wish I could be there and see it all.

KING JAMES. Never mind. You had a first-hand account from me, didn't you?

CONSUELO. These great Church lords - they aren't used to being contradicted. I'd just love to see their faces. Couldn't I just peep from behind a curtain?

KING JAMES. (SMILING) Too much goes on already behind curtains. What would Yolanda say if she caught sight of your face among the tapestries?

CONSUELO. She'd think I was one of the Moorish slaves embroidered in the battle scene.

KING JAMES. No, no. Yolanda is not so easily deceived. You had better keep well out of sight. But tell me, what do you think of the Rabbi?

CONSUELO. He's brave. He has a fire in his soul, even if it comes from hell.

KING JAMES. (FONDLING HER) You like a man to have a fire in his soul, don't you?

CONSUELO. Yes, I do. Why do you think I like you?

KING JAMES. And the other one? Pablo Christiani, our Christian warrior?.

CONSUELO. He takes a long view, that one. Your kingdom is just a stepping-stone to him.

KING JAMES. You're right on that one, you little witch. I recognize ambition when I see it. You know, I should make you my chief counsellor.

HE KISSES HER. ENTER AN ATTENDANT.

ATTENDANT. Your Majesty, it is the urgent request of Rabbi Moses that he be allowed to enter at once.

KING JAMES. Get him. (TO CONSUELO). Stay.

ENTER MOSES BEN NACHMAN.

KING JAMES. Welcome, Rabbi Moses. What is troubling you?

MOSES BEN NACHMAN. Your Majesty, I have come to ask you to put an end to the Disputation.

KING JAMES. Why? You seem to be doing very well.

MOSES BEN NACHMAN. I have come at the request of my people, many of whom have begged me to proceed no further.

KING JAMES. But I am looking forward to more debate. It is as good a contest as I've ever seen.

MOSES BEN NACHMAN. Your Majesty, we have many enemies, especially among the Dominicans. There is a great hatred growing. If we are not now quiet, I fear a disaster may befall us.

KING JAMES. Do you not trust me?

MOSES BEN NACHMAN. If I had not trusted you I would not have opened my mouth in this debate. Your majesty, it's clear that I will not be converted to Christianity. Let the Disputation end.

KING JAMES. Tell me, have the arguments of Pablo Christiani had no effect on you at all?

MOSES BEN NACHMAN. Pablo Christiani is a very slight man.

KING JAMES. And you are a very arrogant man.

MOSES BEN NACHMAN. My concern is for the safety of my fellow Jews.

KING JAMES. I have assured you of the safety of your people. I ask you again, do you not trust me?

MOSES BEN NACHMAN. I do trust you.

KING JAMES. So there is one Christian you can trust?

MOSES BEN NACHMAN. It is not the Christian in you that I trust, your Majesty, but the pagan.

KING JAMES. Am I a pagan?

MOSES BEN NACHMAN. Your sense of justice is not Christian but pagan.

KING JAMES. Raymond de Penaforte is always saying the same thing. I suppose that when both the leading Dominican and the leading Jew say I am a pagan, I should consider it might be true.

MOSES BEN NACHMAN. A pagan likes to see a good fight and a good fight can only be had on equal terms. That is the pagan sense of justice. It is not quite what we Jews mean by justice, but it is not so bad. I am afraid though, that paganism is dying out all over Europe. Christianity is winning.

KING JAMES. Rabbi Moses, Christianity defeated paganism many centuries ago.

MOSES BEN NACHMAN. Only in name. Now it is winning in fact. Soon there will be only one ruler in Christendom, the Pope. And there will be no more fair play for the Jews. I have spoken out. I have had my say. If I am forced to take matters further, even your sense of fair play will be overwhelmed.

KING JAMES. No one will give me orders in Aragon.

MOSES BEN NACHMAN. Not even the Pope?

KING JAMES. Not even the Pope.

THERE IS A REFLECTIVE SILENCE, BEFORE JAMES SPEAKS AGAIN.

KING JAMES. What did you mean when you said, "If I am forced to take matters further ..."?

MOSES BEN NACHMAN. The second part of the Disputation takes me into dangerous ground. Let the Disputation end now and perhaps the danger can be avoided. Will you give the order?

KING JAMES. No. I will say when the Disputation ends. (SILENCE)

RABBI MOSES. Have I your permission to withdraw from your presence?

KING JAMES. Yes.

HE BEGINS TO WITHDRAW, BUT THE KING STOPS HIM.

KING JAMES. Wait a moment. (PAUSE) I want to ask you something.

MOSES BEN NACHMAN. Yes?

KING JAMES. Rabbi, in your religion, can a man ever receive forgiveness for adultery?

MOSES BEN NACHMAN. We had a king once, our greatest king, King David. He committed adultery. But he repented and was forgiven.

KING JAMES. But if a man sins and sins and does not repent because he loves his sin, can he still find forgiveness?

MOSES BEN NACHMAN. No.

KING JAMES. Ah, you see, that is where Jesus is better than your hard God.

MOSES BEN NACHMAN. And what about those we harm by our continued sin? What does Jesus' forgiveness do for them?

KING JAMES. It is the evil body that hinders our salvation.

MOSES BEN NACHMAN. The body is good.

KING JAMES. How can that be, when it is filled with lustful yearnings?

MOSES BEN NACHMAN. These are not bad yearnings, if they are rightly directed.

KING JAMES. Then lust can be good?

MOSES BEN NACHMAN. Was it not created by God? Is it not the movement of the fountain of life? I have written a book about the holiness of sexual desire.

KING JAMES. A book? You are a lewd rabbi, Moses.

RABBI MOSES. A king should take his pleasures like a lion. Our King David had eighteen wives and concubines, and that was reckoned no sin. Only his adultery with Bathsheba was considered a sin, because she was a married woman.

KING JAMES. Eighteen wives and concubines, eh? I should have been a king before Jesus came.

EXIT MOSES. CONSUELO COMES FORWARD. THEY KISS.

KING JAMES. We shouldn't do this. It is a sin.

CONSUELO. You have your confessor. Confess tomorrow.

SHE KISSES HIM. HE IS COLD.

KING JAMES. I grow old. It is a sign from God to repent.

CONSUELO. You are not old. You are James the Conqueror. Don't let anyone persuade you to die before your time. You have the power.

Don't let them take it away from you. But I'll leave you now. You rest. (PAUSE) You know I do love you.

EXIT CONSUELO. LIGHTS CHANGE. RABBI MOSES WAITS. RAYMOND DE PENAFORTE ENTERS.

SCENE FOUR

RAYMOND DE PENAFORTE.   Thank you for coming, Rabbi.

MOSES BEN NACHMAN.   Not at all. I am happy to cooperate.

RAYMOND DE PENAFORTE.   Well, the Disputation is drawing to a close. It has, I'm afraid, been a disappointment to me. I had hoped that by our taking a gentle approach, Christians and Jews could enter into friendly relations. Unfortunately, Rabbi, you have not returned gentleness for gentleness.

MOSES BEN NACHMAN.   What is it that you propose, Brother Raymond?

RAYMOND DE PENAFORTE.   All we ask is that you adopt a more conciliatory tone. Defend Judaism, by all means, but do not attack Christianity. Perhaps you can now see the wisdom of my original proposal of placing restrictions on our Disputation.

MOSES BEN NACHMAN.   What you say sounds very reasonable, Brother Raymond, but how can one defend Judaism without attacking Christianity?

RAYMOND DE PENAFORTE.   We have tried to be fair. Would you prefer a Disputation like the one in Paris where they burnt the Talmud? We have made progress.

MOSES BEN NACHMAN.   I agree. We have made progress. But aren't you really saying to me, "Since we are for once allowing you to say what you think, show your gratitude by not saying what you think." This kind of tolerance keeps our mouths shut as well as any intolerance.

RAYMOND DE PENAFORTE.   You may say what you think without attacking Christianity.

MOSES BEN NACHMAN.   I cannot guarantee that.

RAYMOND DE PENAFORTE. But why?

MOSES BEN NACHMAN. I feel that this is an historic occasion. This is the only time in a very long age that there has been a frank meeting between Jews and Christians. Who knows when such an occasion may occur again? I do not think that we are entering a new era of tolerance. Only here in Barcelona, under a fair king, do we have a fleeting moment of true contact. But how can a man on trial defend himself without casting doubt on the prosecutor's case? What Christians experience as an insolent attack on their religion is simply the struggle of the Jew to clear himself of the charges levelled against him by Christians.

RAYMOND DE PENAFORTE. There have been no charges levelled against you.

MOSES BEN NACHMAN. (WITH PASSION) Do you not accuse us of being the murderers of God? Is not this why we are hounded in Christendom? There was a time when the common people did not hate the Jews. They came to our wedding feasts and asked the rabbis to bless their fields. Now they have been told so many times by Christian priests that the Jews are God-murderers that they have come to believe every abominable story about us - that we poison wells and drink the blood of Christian children. These stories have led to massacres in Germany and France. Only with God's help will we escape extermination in Christendom.

RAYMOND DE PENAFORTE. This is all an unfortunate popular misunderstanding. The Pope has done his best to combat these barbaric stories.

MOSES BEN NACHMAN. If Pope Urban were really doing his best he would make every priest warn his congregation of these lies every Sunday for a thousand Sundays, and that would be a start to the end of the persecution.

RAYMOND DE PENAFORTE. The Jews did bring about the death of Christ, but not because they were especially wicked. All of us are guilty of it. The Jews just happened to represent sinful humanity at that time.

MOSES BEN NACHMAN. If the death of Jesus was merely that of some saintly man, this explanation might have a chance of being accepted by Christians. After all, the Athenians executed Socrates, and still retained the respect of mankind. But Jesus is regarded by you as God. His killers must be devils. Only a devil can be strong enough to kill a god. Worse still, the death of Jesus was not just a tragic event, caused by a wicked crime. It was a necessary event that brought about the salvation of mankind. So the Jews are accused of killing and creating your messiah in the same deadly moment. This fills people with horror and dread for the Jews, and awe - and the awe just adds to the dread. We Jews are ordinary people. But how can Christians accept that, even begin to accept that, when you fill their minds with this violent drama?

RAYMOND DE PENAFORTE.   The Jews are responsible for that. You do not think of yourselves as ordinary people.

MOSES BEN NACHMAN.   True, we think we are the chosen people. But this does not in any way make us supernatural. We like to think of ourselves as leaders of humanity through the desert that is our world, just as Moses, who was a fallible, erring, ordinary human being, led us through the desert. If we Jews reject the role thrust upon us by Christianity, then there is trouble for us.

RAYMOND DE PENAFORTE.   You cannot deny that the Jews killed Jesus.

MOSES BEN NACHMAN.   I do deny it. But that is merely a historical question, and not the point. The point is whether the death of the Jew Jesus is to be worked up into a fantasy about the sacrificial death of a divine being performed by satanic executioners - Jews, devils!

RAYMOND DE PENAFORTE.   A fantasy? That is what you call the Christian scheme of salvation?

MOSES BEN NACHMAN.   I am forced to speak bluntly.

RAYMOND DE PENAFORTE.   Your criticisms of Christianity go very much deeper that those you made in the Disputation. I can see that now.

MOSES BEN NACHMAN.   Surely your own intelligence should tell you that the Jews have refused to accept Christianity because the Jews see something wrong with Christianity. Instead you prefer to think of us as wilfully blind and obstinate, and then you are shocked to the core when we turn out to have reasoned objections to your faith.

RAYMOND DE PENAFORTE. Will you or will you not exercise restraint for the rest of the Disputation?

MOSES BEN NACHMAN. Since you now know the depth of my feelings, you should realise that I have shown great restraint already.

RAYMOND DE PENAFORTE. You should know that your only ally is the King. Beware, Rabbi, it is not safe. The people are simple souls. You seem to be attacking their faith, and this makes them very angry. They dare not give expression to this anger violently, because the King keeps them in tight control. But we must think of the future. The King will not live for ever, and the memory of this Disputation will outlast him. I know you are a wise man, Rabbi, and can see further than the joy of making debating points.

MOSES BEN NACHMAN. So what do you suggest, Brother Raymond? You want me to give the impression that I am seriously considering conversion to Christianity?

RAYMOND DE PENAFORTE. No, no, I do not go as far as that. We all know that you have no intention of giving up your faith. But at least give the impression that it would not be an act of sheer folly or madness for a Jew to become a Christian.

MOSES BEN NACHMAN. You want me to indicate to my fellow-Jews that I would not entirely condemn them if they, or some of them, became converted?

RAYMOND DE PENAFORTE. Something like that.

MOSES BEN NACHMAN. (AFTER A SILENCE) Why do you ask me this?

RAYMOND DE PENAFORTE. I will be frank with you. It is important that we Dominicans should gain some credit from this Disputation. In fact, it is imperative.

MOSES BEN NACHMAN. That is hardly my concern, Brother Raymond.

RAYMOND DE PENAFORTE. Ah, you are mistaken. It is your concern.

MOSES BEN NACHMAN. Why is that?

RAYMOND DE PENAFORTE. The King's position is on a knife edge. Powerful interests wish to dislodge him. His Holiness the Pope is supporting the King at present, but the outcome of the Disputation could affect his attitude. There is strong pressure for Jewish policy in Aragon to conform with that of France. If the King were removed, your position would be very precarious. We have to be able to say that we made at least some progress. We cannot appear weak.

MOSES BEN NACHMAN. It is remarkable how similar your arguments are to those of my own Jewish advisers.

RAYMOND DE PENAFORTE. Ah, there you are. I knew that I could count on some prudence on your side. I am not asking for much - just an alteration of tone. Something to build on when we come to write our report.

MOSES BEN NACHMAN. Your report?

RAYMOND DE PENAFORTE. Oh, yes, there will have to be a report. You need not worry too much about it. Naturally, it will give a certain gloss on the Disputation. You probably will not agree with everything in our report, but all we require of you is that there be no open contradiction.

MOSES BEN NACHMAN. I understand.

RAYMOND DE PENAFORTE. Good. Please understand too that I have no personal feeling against you. But if you do not cooperate, my hand may be forced. Things will happen which I will not be able to prevent.

MOSES BEN NACHMAN. I understand.

RAYMOND DE PENAFORTE. I hope that this visit has not been without benefit.

LIGHTS FADE OUT ON RAYMOND DE PENAFORTE, AS MOSES CROSSES TO THE OTHER SIDE OF THE STAGE.

SCENE FIVE

DISPUTATION SCENE. KING, QUEEN, PABLO, RAYMOND, MOSES, COURTIERS.

RAYMOND DE PENAFORTE. We now proceed to the second question of the Disputation. Is the Messiah spoken of in the Bible and the Talmud divine, or human?

MOSES BEN NACHMAN. Your Majesty, may I raise an objection?.

KING JAMES. (DISPLEASED) An objection?

MOSES BEN NACHMAN. Yes, your Majesty. I cannot see how we can proceed to the second question.

KING JAMES. Why not?

MOSES BEN NACHMAN. Since Brother Pablo was unable to convince me that the Messiah has come, what is the point of discussing whether he has to be divine or not?

KING JAMES. Brother Pablo?

PABLO CHRISTIANI. Since this is one of the main points at issue between Christians and Jews, as Rabbi Moses himself agreed at the beginning, why should we not discuss it?

MOSES BEN NACHMAN. But surely the whole point of this Disputation is to claim that Jesus was the Messiah.

PABLO CHRISTIANI. Not at all, your Majesty. We are discussing the Messiah in general, rather than Jesus in particular. We are trying to discover, in the abstract and on the basis of texts, first whether the Messiah has come, and secondly, whether his nature is divine. The two questions can be discussed quite separately.

MOSES BEN NACHMAN. Surely you are not trying to convince me about some Messiah who has come and is divine but who is other than Jesus?

PABLO CHRISTIANI. The Rabbi is putting up an unconvincing pretence of being simple-minded. Certainly everything we discuss has a bearing on Jesus. But we are approaching Jesus indirectly. As I said, we are talking about the Messiah in general. Jews will never be able to accept Jesus as long as they do not understand what kind of Messiah to expect.

MOSES BEN NACHMAN. Thank you, Brother Pablo, for your reply. It was very helpful. We can take it, then, that for the sake of our discussion, we are not talking about Jesus, but only about the Messiah in general?

PABLO CHRISTIANI. That is so.

MOSES BEN NACHMAN. Good. I wanted that to be clear. So that whatever I say may not be held to be directed against any person or persons regarded as most sacred by Christians. I enter into this second part of the Disputation very reluctantly, but I am glad it is now so clearly established that we are talking about texts, not about persons.

KING JAMES. Well, if that is quite settled, let's get on. Brother Pablo.

PABLO CHRISTIANI. Thank you, your Majesty. We are all familiar with the arguments based on the Old Testament on which we Christians found our belief that the Messiah is divine. We are familiar also with the arguments by which the Jews attempt to explain away these texts. But they may not be able to explain away the texts I am going to quote from the Talmud. These texts show clearly that the Talmud expects a divine Messiah, not a mere mortal earthly ruler, sitting on the throne of David and Solomon in Jerusalem, as the Jews claim. The Talmud says (PAUSE, AND THEN WITH GREAT EMPHASIS) that the Messiah will sit at the right hand of God. (PAUSE FOR EFFECT) How can a mere mortal sit at the right hand of God? How can the Messiah sit at the right hand of God the Father, if he is sitting on a throne in Jerusalem?

KING JAMES. What have you to say to this, Rabbi?

MOSES BEN NACHMAN. Does God have a right hand?.

PABLO CHRISTIANI. Not literally, no, but in some spiritual sense, yes, or the Talmud would not speak of it. Our Christian scriptures too speak of Jesus sitting at the right hand of God.

MOSES BEN NACHMAN. Well, I see you did not mention that this relationship is found in the Hebrew Bible too, not just in the Talmud.

PABLO CHRISTIANI. Yes, of course. It is in the Psalms. "The Lord said to my Lord: Sit thou at my right hand." But I quoted it from the Talmud instead, to show you how the Talmud, on which our Disputation is based, affirms that this refers to the Messiah.

MOSES BEN NACHMAN. You are indeed a great student of the Talmud, Brother Pablo, to have discovered this amazing passage.

PABLO CHRISTIANI. I do not claim to be a great Talmudist, Rabbi. I merely claim that the great Talmudists among the Jews, including yourself, need to have their attention drawn to certain obvious passages.

MOSES BEN NACHMAN. Obvious, yes. Did you read the whole passage in the Talmud, or only the first few words of it?

PABLO IS SILENT.

MOSES BEN NACHMAN. If you had read on a little further, you would have seen where it says that Abraham will sit at God's left hand. Are you arguing that Abraham too is divine? You see you expect our gratitude because you treat the Talmud as a holy book. But you must also treat it as a sensible book, and not pick out passages at random from it, without regard to their context.

RAYMOND DE PENAFORTE. Why are you so dismissive, Rabbi Moses? I am disappointed in you. Why can we not discuss the Talmud together like brothers? Do you not see that we regard it as holy, just like the Old Testament? We have based our whole case on Judaism, and spoken almost as if we were Jews ourselves. What we are saying to you is, 'Forget about this gulf you see between us. We are all children of Abraham.'

MOSES BEN NACHMAN. Very commendable, yes. But allow me to question this admirable claim. You are saying that you are the true Jews, and we are only pretending to be Jews.

RAYMOND DE PENAFORTE. What do you mean?.

MOSES BEN NACHMAN. First you appropriated our Bible, and now you want to appropriate our Talmud too.

RAYMOND DE PENAFORTE. They are not yours, they are God's.

MOSES BEN NACHMAN. For a long time you said to us, 'We Christians know what the Bible means, and you Jews do not.' Now you are adding another claim, 'We Christians know what the Talmud means, and you Jews do not.' First you turn us out of one heritage, and now you want to turn us out of another. I say that we

Jews, who were given the Bible, or what you call the Old Testament, by God, and who created the Talmud by our own labour over many centuries, know best how to interpret them both.

RAYMOND DE PENAFORTE. And where does that leave us Christians?

MOSES BEN NACHMAN. You must find some way of being Christians that does not exclude us from being Jews.

RAYMOND DE PENAFORTE. I am afraid that you are excluding us from being Christians, Rabbi Moses. You have gone too far.

KING JAMES. (TO MOSES) Continue your argument.

MOSES BEN NACHMAN. The passage in the Talmud - the whole passage in the Talmud - to which Brother Pablo refers reads, `In time to come the Holy One, blessed be He, will seat the Messiah on his right hand and Abraham on his left. (HE TURNS TO PABLO) I repeat my question. Why did you omit what the Talmud says about Abraham?

PABLO IS SILENT.

MOSES BEN NACHMAN. If the Messiah is divine because he sits at God's right hand, what does that make Abraham? Divine too? It seems that you are rather selective in what you quote from the Talmud, Brother Pablo. Was it this great Talmudic insight that caused you to bid the King to assemble before you the sages of the Jews to hold a Disputation over your discoveries?. Was it this great Talmudic insight that made you turn from a Jew to a Christian?.

PABLO. (COLDLY FURIOUS) No, it was because I encountered my divine Lord, Jesus Christ. Who was born from a virgin, a miraculous birth that proves him to be the son of no mortal man, but of God Himself. (PAUSE) Tell me, Rabbi Moses, do you acknowledge that Isaiah prophesies the miraculous birth of the Messiah from a virgin?

MOSES BEN NACHMAN. Isaiah? I thought we were talking about the Talmud. Can't you find a passage in the Talmud that says that the Messiah will be born of a virgin? (TURNING TO THE KING) Your Majesty, he is bringing in the case of Jesus, though it was agreed that we would discuss only the Messiah in general.

PABLO CHRISTIANI. It was merely incidental. I am asking you: is it not prophesied that the Messiah would be born of a virgin, and does this not prove him to be divine?

MOSES BEN NACHMAN. There was no such prophecy.

PABLO CHRISTIANI. But Isaiah says plainly, "A virgin will conceive ...".

MOSES BEN NACHMAN. In your translation, yes. But the Hebrew does not say "virgin". The Hebrew is almah, which means simply "young woman", not virgin. The Hebrew for "virgin" is another word, betulah. Nevertheless, even if a child was born of a virgin, what would that prove? It would not prove the child divine, only that God had performed a miracle. God can perform any miracle -- he could cause a child to be born of a stone, if He wanted. He caused Isaac to be born of a ninety-year old woman, Sarah, but that does not make Isaac divine.

PABLO CHRISTIANI. So Jesus may have been born of a virgin? And yet that would not prove him to be divine?

MOSES BEN NACHMAN. He has gone back to Jesus again.

KING JAMES. The point concerns the Messiah in general. Answer him.

MOSES BEN NACHMAN. God can perform any miracle. Lazarus rose from the dead, but even your Scripture does not argue that Lazarus was therefore divine. One should not confuse miracles with divinity.

PABLO CHRISTIANI. This is very interesting. Do you really think then that Jesus may have been born miraculously and resurrected miraculously?

MOSES BEN NACHMAN. No, I don't think that. I think he was born and died like any other person.

PABLO CHRISTIANI. If Jesus was not born miraculously, does that make his mother a whore?

GREAT STIR IN THE AUDIENCE. MOSES IS TAKEN ABACK. PABLO CONTINUES RELENTLESSLY.

PABLO CHRISTIANI. We know that Joseph was not his father. You say that God was not his father. You deny even that his birth was miraculous. Where does that leave his mother, Our Lady the Virgin Mary?

MOSES BEN NACHMAN. Your Majesty ...

PABLO. (INTERRUPTING ANGRILY) Do you think I don't know what the Jews say about Jesus? That he was a bastard, and his mother was an adulteress? What do you have to say about that?.

MOSES BEN NACHMAN. Brother Pablo has made a serious allegation. I am not obliged to answer it, because it concerns the persons of Jesus and his mother Mary, and we agreed that this Disputation was to be about texts, not persons. But if unanswered, his allegation may cause harm to my people, so I wish to comment on it.

KING JAMES. Go ahead.

MOSES BEN NACHMAN. We Jews do not regard Jesus as a bastard. Nor do we regard Mary as an adulteress.

KING JAMES. Who was the father of Jesus, then?

MOSES BEN NACHMAN. Joseph.

KING JAMES. But the Gospels say that he was not the father.

MOSES BEN NACHMAN. The Gospels are Christian works which we Jews are not bound to believe.

PABLO CHRISTIANI. He denies the virginity of Mary as well as the divinity of Christ!.

MOSES BEN NACHMAN. I am a Jew, and hold Jewish beliefs. But we do not hold insulting beliefs about the persons sacred in your religion. Both Joseph and Mary, in our view, were good people. Nor do we venerate virginity, as you do. For lifelong virgins, we have nothing but pity. Mary was not a virgin, but a good Jewish mother who bore a child to her husband Joseph. It was you Christians who denied Joseph's paternity, so throwing quite unnecessary doubt on Jesus' legitimacy.

KING JAMES. Rabbi, you deny one charge of blasphemy only to admit others almost as bad.

MOSES BEN NACHMAN. Well, your Majesty, if I believed in your Christian doctrines, why should you go to all the trouble and expense of holding a Disputation to convert me? I admit disbelief; I don't admit being insulting.

RAYMOND DE PENAFORTE. Your Majesty, this Disputation has been diverted from its purpose.

KING JAMES. It has certainly taken some unexpected turns. Let's get back to discussing Talmudic texts. Brother Pablo.

PABLO CHRISTIANI. The Talmud says that the Messiah existed before the creation of the world. (PAUSE) How can this be unless he is divine?

MOSES BEN NACHMAN. You have misread the text, Brother Pablo. It says that the thought of the Messiah existed in the mind of God before the creation of the world. How could God create the world without a plan? The Messiah is the culmination of God's plan for the world.

PABLO CHRISTIANI. (EAGERLY) How can the Messiah be a mere man, if he is, as you say, the culmination of God's plan for the world? How can the world be saved by a man?

MOSES BEN NACHMAN. The Messiah does not save the world. The world must save itself by turning to the light of God's teaching. Then the Messiah will come.

PABLO CHRISTIANI. How can man save himself?

MOSES BEN NACHMAN. How else can he be saved?

PABLO CHRISTIANI. Man is helpless. He is sunk in the sin of the Fall of Adam. The coming of the Christ Messiah was to save him and now he is saved in the great body of Christ, the Church. Outside that, he is lost!

MOSES BEN NACHMAN. When Adam sinned he sinned for himself, not for me. Adam was a man and I am a man and each of us is responsible for his own sins, and for nobody else's. Why should I be damned for Adam's sin? Or need a divine Messiah to come and rescue me? Or need a Mother Church to climb back into her womb?

PABLO WALKS ABOUT IN SILENT FURY. THEN HE MAKES A DECISION, AND SPEAKS.

PABLO CHRISTIANI. If Jesus was not divine, what was he? A devil?

MOSES BEN NACHMAN. No.

PABLO CHRISTIANI. You say that he deceived mankind by claiming to be God. He must therefore be a deceiving devil!

MOSES BEN NACHMAN. Your Majesty, he is breaking our agreement again! He must speak about the Messiah in general, not about Jesus.

PABLO CHRISTIANI. Jesus claimed to be God. Either he was God, or he was a liar. Which do you choose, Rabbi Moses?

MOSES BEN NACHMAN. (PLEADING) Your Majesty ...

KING JAMES. Answer the question, Rabbi Moses.

THERE IS A LONG SILENCE.

KING JAMES. Rabbi Moses?

MOSES BEN NACHMAN. I choose silence.

KING JAMES. You what?

MOSES BEN NACHMAN. I refuse to answer.

LONG PAUSE.

KING JAMES. Will you please explain why you refuse to answer?

MOSES BEN NACHMAN. Because ... (HE STRUGGLES WITH HIMSELF) Because ...

KING JAMES. Yes?

MOSES BEN NACHMAN. (HIS FACE WORKING WITH RELUCTANCE) Because I am not competent to answer that question.

KING JAMES. Not competent?

MOSES BEN NACHMAN. My studies have all been in our Jewish books, your Majesty. I am not competent to answer questions about the New Testament. You must find some other Jewish scholar who has investigated the matter more fully than I have.

KING JAMES. Well, this is most unexpected modesty on your part, Rabbi Moses.

MOSES BEN NACHMAN. I am ready to answer any question about Jewish beliefs on the Messiah. I cannot be expected to know how these beliefs relate to Christian ideas.

PABLO CHRISTIANI. Your Majesty, this is mere subterfuge. He keeps silence because he does not want to incriminate himself and his fellow-Jews by disclosing their hatred and contempt of our Lord.

KING JAMES. Is this true, Rabbi?

MOSES BEN NACHMAN. I have nothing to say.

RAYMOND DE PENAFORTE. (COMING FORWARD) Your majesty, I do not think that Rabbi Moses should be pressed in this way.

PABLO CHRISTIANI. I cannot accept this.

KING JAMES. (AMUSED) You are rebelling against your superior?

PABLO CHRISTIANI. Brother Raymond has all my respect, but he put me in charge of the Christian case here, and I must pursue it in my own way. It is not sufficient to discuss texts. We must expose the whole Jewish heresy.

KING JAMES. Heresy? I thought Judaism was a permitted religion?

PABLO CHRISTIANI. Ideas on that can change.

RAYMOND DE PENAFORTE. No, they must not change. The Jews are our roots, the guardians of the Old Testament, on which we base our faith. They must be converted by persuasion, not by force. They must not be harmed.

KING JAMES. Rabbi Moses, do you still wish to remain silent?

MOSES BEN NACHMAN. Yes, your Majesty.

KING JAMES.   Do you still plead incompetence to reply?

MOSES BEN NACHMAN.   Yes, your Majesty.

PABLO CHRISTIANI.   Your Majesty, it is clear that this Disputation is a total victory for the Christian side. The Jewish participant has been reduced to silence, and even admits that he is unable to answer the question put to him.

KING JAMES.   Do you admit defeat, Rabbi Moses?

MOSES BEN NACHMAN.   No.

KING JAMES.   But you have been reduced to silence!

MOSES BEN NACHMAN.   Only on a question that is outside the limits of the Disputation.

RAYMOND DE PENAFORTE.   This is true, your Majesty.

PABLO CHRISTIANI.   If he does not accept defeat, the only conclusion we can reach is that he knows that his reply would be a blasphemy. He fears the consequences if he speaks out.

MOSES BEN NACHMAN. (AFTER A SILENCE)   Your Majesty, whether I am silent or speak, the result could be dangerous to your Jewish subjects.

RAYMOND DE PENAFORTE.   Remain silent.

KING JAMES.   I have guaranteed his safety. Speak.

MOSES BEN NACHMAN. (RESIGNEDLY)   I will speak then. I wish to say emphatically that I do not regard Jesus as a cheat or a devil, but as a good man.

PABLO CHRISTIANI.   How can that be? Did he not claim to be God? What you are saying is that he deceived mankind by claiming to be God. He must then be a deceiving devil.

MOSES BEN NACHMAN.   My study of your New Testament has shown me that Jesus never claimed to be God. The Church has perverted his teaching into idolatry.

SHOCK, HORROR.

PABLO CHRISTIANI. Is Christianity then idolatry?.

MOSES BEN NACHMAN. The first commandment says, "Thou shalt have no other Gods before me". To worship a man as God is idolatry. The same idolatry of which the Egyptians were guilty when they worshipped the man Pharaoh, and the Romans when they worshipped the man Caesar.

UPROAR. CRIES OF "KILL HIM", "BURN THE BLASPHEMER".

MOSES BEN NACHMAN. (IGNORING THE CRIES. HE SPEAKS IN A TONE OF CALM LEGAL ARGUMENT) Some Rabbis hold, however, that Christianity, since it is based on the Bible and does not perform idolatrous rites as defined in the Talmud, is not idolatry, but merely a heresy of Judaism.

RAYMOND DE PENAFORTE. (ENTERING THE LIGHT) Merely a heresy!

UPROAR IN THE AUDIENCE. KING JAMES RAISES HIS HAND ANGRILY.

KING JAMES. Silence!

THERE IS INSTANT SILENCE. THE LIGHTS CHANGE.

SCENE SIX

KING JAMES, RAYMOND, QUEEN YOLANDA, PABLO.

RAYMOND DE PENAFORTE. I am afraid the matter is out of hand.

KING JAMES. How do you mean?

RAYMOND DE PENAFORTE. The Rabbi has said things that should never have been allowed to be said. Under any circumstances.

KING JAMES. Come, come, Raymond. Don't exaggerate. It is only a debate.

RAYMOND DE PENAFORTE. I'm afraid you don't understand, your Majesty. The Rabbi has uttered blasphemy in public. Under Church law, the punishment for that is death.

KING JAMES.   But I gave him permission to speak his mind.

RAYMOND DE PENAFORTE.   Indeed you did, your Majesty. But that does not affect the legal situation.

KING JAMES. (ANGRY)   Don't tell me what the legal situation is. I am the law in Aragon.

RAYMOND DE PENAFORTE.   Indeed you are, your Majesty. You are the secular law and you have the power of life and death. It is also your responsibility to implement Church law and Church law requires a penalty of death for blasphemy.

KING JAMES.   He did not want to blaspheme. He wanted to remain silent.

RAYMOND DE PENAFORTE.   I quite agree. I regret Brother Pablo's method of interrogation. Nevertheless, the blasphemy has now occurred.

KING JAMES.   Has it occurred to you, Raymond, that many of the things that have been said on our side of the Disputation strike the Jews as blasphemous?

SILENCE.

RAYMOND DE PENAFORTE. (WITH AN EFFORT)   You are very fair, your Majesty. But I would like to remind you that your desire for fair play, which would be most commendable in less urgent circumstances, may lead you directly into hell-fire.

KING JAMES.   Is fair play, then, not a Christian virtue?

RAYMOND DE PENAFORTE.   Within certain limits, yes. But as an absolute concept, it is pagan.

KING JAMES.   I gave my word to Rabbi Moses that he would be allowed to put forward any argument he felt necessary to his case, and that there would be no reprisals.

QUEEN YOLANDA.   Your word to a Jew?

KING JAMES GIVES HER A LOOK OF SILENT CONTEMPT.

QUEEN YOLANDA. But are you not shocked? Have you ever heard such sheer wickedness? I thought that it was obstinacy that made them refuse to acknowledge Christ. The truth is far worse. They regard us as heretics and idolaters!

PABLO CHRISTIANI. Your Majesty's exaggerated sense of fair play has given the Jew the opportunity to spit on the wounds of Christ. Yet at least we now see exactly where we are.

KING JAMES. If you want a fight, you should expect to see some blows delivered. I cannot see that the Jew has said anything out of a mere desire to blaspheme.

RAYMOND DE PENAFORTE. (LOSING HIS COMPOSURE) Which side are you on?

KING JAMES. (GIVING HIM A STARE) You forget yourself, Raymond.

RAYMOND DE PENAFORTE. I apologise, your Majesty. I spoke too heatedly out of my great zeal. But we have to consider the safety of the Jews themselves. If nothing is done to punish Rabbi Moses, there may be some outbreaks of violence.

KING JAMES. (SUDDENLY IN A TOWERING RAGE) Outbreaks of violence? I am still King in Aragon! No one is going to take the law into his own hands in my kingdom!

EXIT KING JAMES.

ALL ARE SILENT FOR A WHILE.

RAYMOND DE PENAFORTE. The King will not yield. This is your doing, Pablo. Conflict between the King and the Pope is now inevitable.

QUEEN YOLANDA. But the King has not stopped the proceedings. The Rabbi has been shaken. He must be aware of the danger he is in. Now is the time, Pablo, to convert him.

LIGHTS UP. DISPUTATION RESUMES.

PABLO CHRISTIANI. For my final argument, let us leave the interpretation of texts, and turn to the teaching of our Lord Jesus Christ himself.

Remember the story of the Pharisee and the tax-gatherer who stood side by side in prayer. The Pharisee said as he prayed, "Thank God I am not as other men are." But the tax-gatherer smote upon his breast and said, "God be merciful to me, a sinner." And Christ tells us that the sinner, not the Pharisee, was justified in the eyes of God. That is the difference between Christianity and Judaism. He who looks into his own heart and is appalled by the corruption he finds there knows that without a Saviour he is lost. To look into the abyss of Hell and be appalled - that is the beginning of wisdom. Your religion is for the chosen few, the elite. It does not answer to the need in the heart of every man. That is why the Christian Church gains new converts every day; that is why it will conquer the world. Christians stand poised between heaven and hell, with the pit at our feet and our arms outstretched to our Saviour, who draws us up from the brink of destruction.

But the Jews say that the Messiah is only a man and he does not bring salvation. They say that they do not need salvation, because of their learning and practice of their law, the Torah. I beg Rabbi Moses to reflect that this is superficial, arrogant and complacent.

(TOWARDS MOSES) Do not think of yourself as a Rabbi, a great and learned man above the common herd. Think of yourself only as a human being, and say, with tears, "God be merciful to me, a sinner." Then you will understand the need for our divine saviour.

(TO EVERYONE) I pray that with God's help I may have touched the heart of the Jew. (THERE IS A LONG PAUSE)

MOSES BEN NACHMAN. Superficial, arrogant, complacent. These are the charges Brother Pablo brings against Judaism. These are heavy charges. To acknowledge one's sinfulness is certainly a great thing. But shall we go further and call ourselves worthless? Were we not created in the image of God? And is it not an insult to God, who created us, to call ourselves worthless? Self-criticism is good, and where can you find more examples of this than in our Jewish writings? What other nation has put on record in its sacred book every backsliding, every weakness, every sin and disloyalty of which it has been guilty? And our enemies are not slow to use this record against us. But blessed is the nation that is not afraid to reveal its faults to its enemies. Let us consider what the aim of humility is. Is it not to learn by one's errors and do better in the future? But if humility is carried to such a point that one says, "I am utterly worthless, no action of mine can ever be good, only divine intervention can save me," then the incentive for improvement has been destroyed. Excessive humility then becomes an excuse for lack of effort. Is this not what you Christians do?

RAYMOND DE PENAFORTE. Take care!

MOSES BEN NACHMAN. You ask God to take you over, and you give up the task for which He put you in the world, like a child who refuses to walk.

AN ANGRY RUMBLING PERMEATES THE GALLERY.

MOSES BEN NACHMAN. Then something far worse happens: you believe that your Saviour has snatched you from the abyss into a state of sinlessness in which you believe you can do nothing wrong. From a state of abject humility, you emerge into a state of incredible arrogance, and proclaim that you are saved, and that God now speaks from your mouth!

IN THE GALLERY THE ANGER GROWS.

MOSES BEN NACHMAN. We Jews know that no man on this earth is ever without sin, not Moses, and yes, not even the Messiah. We must grapple with the evil inclination from the first day of our lives to the last. Is this our complacency? We Jews are proud, but we want all men to be proud. We were chosen by God, but for what? For power? For happiness? For rest and security in our possessions? For ease and comfort? No! For pain and misery and persecution and wandering over the face of the earth! Do not say that we have not seen the abyss. We are on the brink of an abyss of destruction every day of our lives, and in every generation we face those who would like to rid the earth of us. Ever since we began our journey when we crossed the desert with only a pillar of fire to guide us, we have seen the abyss. Yet we continue our journey to the Promised Land of peace and brotherhood on earth in the age of the Messiah.

UPROAR. THE LIGHTS CHANGE.

SCENE SEVEN

KING JAMES, QUEEN YOLANDA.

QUEEN YOLANDA. You have behaved very badly, James.

KING JAMES. What do you mean?

QUEEN YOLANDA. You have treated the Jew with quite unnecessary favour

KING JAMES. Well, I don't care who knows it. In my opinion, the Jew won the Disputation with a good many points to spare.

QUEEN YOLANDA. Why don't you become a Jew, then?

KING JAMES. Eh? Become a Jew? Don't be ridiculous.

QUEEN YOLANDA. Since you found the Jew so convincing.

KING JAMES. One doesn't decide one's religion on the basis of a few days' verbal fencing. It was just a pleasure to see someone fighting with words instead of broadswords.

QUEEN YOLANDA. Not everyone took the view that the Jew had the best of it. You actually gave him a prize.

KING JAMES. Not exactly a prize, Yolanda. Just a token of my esteem. Just a few gold coins,

QUEEN YOLANDA. 300 gold crowns! What prompted such a magnanimous gesture?

KING JAMES. Respect. Never had I heard so unjust a cause so skilfully argued.

QUEEN YOLANDA. He may come to regret his free and easy manner of arguing on holy topics.

KING JAMES. Yolanda! I warn you, do not plot against the Rabbi.

QUEEN YOLANDA. Plot? There is no need. Things will merely take their course, in God's good time. This is by no means the end of the matter.

SCENE EIGHT

MOSES BEN NACHMAN'S HOME. LOUD KNOCKING. VOICE FROM OUTSIDE.

MOSES BEN NACHMAN.   But as you say, spoken words vanish in the wind.

PABLO CHRISTIANI.   There is still time to recant.

MOSES BEN NACHMAN.   No.

PABLO CHRISTIANI.   Are you in love with death, Rabbi?

MOSES BEN NACHMAN.   No, we are forbidden to court death. But there are times when we are commanded to risk death.

PABLO CHRISTIANI.   You are facing death. What use are your Talmudic arguments now?

MOSES BEN NACHMAN.   Many disciples of the Talmud have faced death before me. They faced it with courage.

PABLO CHRISTIANI.   If they found courage, it was in spite of the Talmud, not because of it. What is there in the Talmud to help a man on the brink of death?

MOSES BEN NACHMAN.   The Talmud is about life, not death. But those who love life best, I find, know best how to die.

PABLO CHRISTIANI.   Rabbi Moses, you cannot tell me you are satisfied. A man with a great soul like you.

MOSES BEN NACHMAN.   What do you want from me?

PABLO CHRISTIANI.   How can you carry on calmly when the world is a nightmare? I studied the Talmud and found it full of the sayings and stories of the rabbis. But what do we really know about the rabbis of the Talmud? Where is their heart-ache, their doubt, their terror, their bewilderment, their black despair? Nowhere. Instead there is a calm atmosphere of minute discussion, as if the world were always at noontime on a mild summer's day. Then I look into the Christian Bible, the New Testament, and I find agony and despair - "My God, my God, why hast thou forsaken me?" - and doubt and bewilderment - "Who shall deliver me from the body of this death?" This speaks to me. This is life as I find it, not the untroubled certainties of the rabbis.

MOSES BEN NACHMAN.   And when did you become convinced that

the world is a nightmare?.

PABLO CHRISTIANI.   When I saw my father and mother killed in the massacre in France. When I lay in hiding and saw them torn to pieces, and could do nothing. When I saw the entire Jewish quarter destroyed after being accused of attacking a communion wafer.

MOSES BEN NACHMAN.   And this, you think, is the reality of life, good Brother Pablo?

PABLO CHRISTIANI.   It is. Not the academies of the Jews, in which they debate about the egg which was laid on a festival day. What help is that to a person in despair? I can tell you from my own experience as a Jew that Judaism has nothing to say to such a person. I need a religion that knows how to deal with a crisis; a religion that regards life itself as a crisis - whose symbol is a man in agony on a cross.

MOSES BEN NACHMAN.   Was it not Christian zeal that killed your father and mother?.

PABLO CHRISTIANI.   Christianity was not responsible. It is life, that is all. Is it Christianity that causes famines, or wars? Is it Christianity that causes the evil in the heart of man? You have no way of coping with evil. Oh, you suffer all evils, but you learn nothing from them, thinking them temporary inconveniences interrupting your studies. Despite the evil in the world, you think all is well. Christ said he came not for the whole, but for the sick. No one is whole. We are all sick, especially those who think that they are whole.

MOSES BEN NACHMAN.   As a doctor of bodies as well as of souls I can tell you that I would have to give up my profession if I thought all people sick beyond help. We must regard health as normal, sickness as something abnormal. Sickness is to be cured, not accepted. However, some patients, I find, are hard to cure because they find it more interesting to be ill than to be well.

PABLO CHRISTIANI.   Perhaps they are looking for a more radical cure than any you have to offer.

MOSES BEN NACHMAN.   It is a mistake to look for radical cures. There is only one radical cure - death. We must accept the human condition - never quite well, and yet grateful for a modicum of health.

PABLO CHRISTIANI. Death is the radical cure. We must die in order to be reborn!.

MOSES BEN NACHMAN. Lovers of death say that. But I will say this. There are some who cannot be cured by ordinary medicine. Those who have experienced the shock of the vision of evil - there are remedies even for them. (HE LOOKS AT PABLO SYMPATHETICALLY AND HIS VOICE SOFTENS) You should have come to me Pablo, for your sickness and not gone for enlightenment to the very people who brought about the death of your parents.

PABLO CHRISTIANI. (RAGING AND CRYING) You are an arrogant old fool standing in the way of Christ. You could have been a great man. You could have led the Jews to Christianity. Instead you and many other Jews will suffer and die. That is a responsibility you will take to your Maker.

EXIT PABLO CHRISTIANI.

SCENE TEN

MOSES BEN NACHMAN BEFORE KING JAMES.

KING JAMES. You have been condemned to banishment, Rabbi Moses. In view of your recklessness in publishing your own account of the Disputation, this was the best I could do for you. I blocked the attempt to charge you with blasphemy for what you said in the Disputation, but I gave you no permission to write. If I had allowed you to go to your death for that, you would have no cause for complaint. But in view of my personal regard for you, I have exerted myself on your behalf. I hope you understand that I have saved you from death.

MOSES BEN NACHMAN. I do understand, your Majesty, and I am grateful.

KING JAMES. (IN A MORE PERSONAL TONE) You have had a narrow escape, Moses. I cannot understand why you took such a risk. You have risked your life and the well-being of your community. Why so reckless, Moses?

MOSES BEN NACHMAN. In the future, I can see only suffering for us. There will be more Disputations, and they will be conducted more brutally. I wanted to leave my people something to hold on to, a true record of an occasion when for once, under a just King, a Jew was allowed to speak out. Otherwise, all that would be left of the Disputation would be the account put out by the Dominicans.

KING JAMES. I can understand that. I am glad that you are to suffer no more than exile. Where will you go?

MOSES BEN NACHMAN. I have much work to do. I should like to do it in the Holy Land.

KING JAMES. It's a long way to travel.

MOSES BEN NACHMAN. We Jews are used to travelling.

KING JAMES. What work will you do there?.

MOSES BEN NACHMAN. The study of the Torah has been declining there. I will build an academy. And we must build up the Jewish population there.

KING JAMES. What for?

MOSES BEN NACHMAN. In preparation for the coming of the Messiah.

KING JAMES. Will you do all this on your own?

MOSES BEN NACHMAN. No, there will be others. Rabbi Yechiel of Paris will be there. He too was banished after a Disputation. You should be glad, your Majesty. Your Christian Disputations are helping to build up the Jewish settlement in the Land of Israel.

KING JAMES. That was not really my intention. But I am glad you take it in this spirit. (PAUSE) But tell me, Rabbi Moses, how will you make your living?

MOSES BEN NACHMAN. By my profession.

KING JAMES. As a rabbi?

MOSES BEN NACHMAN. No, that is not a profession. I am a physician.

KING JAMES. (SUDDENLY VERY INTERESTED) A physician! (HE

FEELS HIS BACK, THEN CHANGES HIS MIND) No, no matter. (PAUSE) Is there anything more I can do for you, Rabbi Moses?.

MOSES BEN NACHMAN. Only that you should see that no other Jew suffers from this Disputation.

KING JAMES. I shall see to that.

MOSES BEN NACHMAN. You are a good man. But do not become too much of a Christian. Keep some of the pagan in you.

KING JAMES. Goodbye, Rabbi Moses. I am really very sorry to see you go.

MOSES BEN NACHMAN. Goodbye. (HE STARTS TO GO)

KING JAMES. Just one thing, Rabbi ...

MOSES BEN NACHMAN. Yes?

KING JAMES. Give me your blessing.

HE STARTS TO KNEEL, BUT RABBI MOSES RAISES HIM AND PLACES HIS HAND ON THE KING'S HEAD.

MOSES BEN NACHMAN. Yesimecha Hashem keChoresh melekh Paras, melekh tzedek baGoyim.

KING JAMES. What does it mean?

MOSES BEN NACHMAN. May the Lord make you like Cyrus, King of Persia, a righteous king among the gentiles.

KING JAMES. You had to go back a long way for that one, didn't you?

EXIT MOSES BEN NACHMAN.

ENTER QUEEN YOLANDA.

KING JAMES. I have banished him.

QUEEN YOLANDA. God smiles on you, James. The conversions are beginning to happen.(PAUSE) What is it, James?

JAMES. I was just thinking of something Rabbi Moses once said to me - about King David.

QUEEN YOLANDA. You're tired. I'm going to bed, but I shall not be able to sleep.

JAMES. Good night.

QUEEN YOLANDA. We are on the threshold of great things, James. There will be no Muslims, there will be no Jews, only Christians. There will be no separate Christian kingdoms. There will be one great unified Spain. One Spain, cleansed and pure, a holy kingdom, the crown of Christendom, the forerunner of the worldwide domination of Christ!

KING JAMES. Yolanda, you are indeed a remarkable woman.

QUEEN YOLANDA. Good night, James.

EXIT QUEEN YOLANDA.

KING JAMES. I should have been a king before Jesus came.